Creative

Resources

of Art, Brushes, Buildings . . .

Creative
Resources
of Art, Brushes, Buildings . . .

Judy Herr
Yvonne Libby

Delmar Publishers

I(T)P® International Thomson Publishing

Albany • Bonn • Boston • Cincinnati • Detroit • London • Madrid
Melbourne • Mexico City • New York • Pacific Grove • Paris • San Francisco
Singapore • Tokyo • Toronto • Washington

NOTICE TO THE READER

Cover Design by: Ron Sohn

Delmar Staff
Acquisitions Editor: Jay S. Whitney
Associate Editor: Erin O'Connor-Traylor
Developmental Editor: Ellen Smith
Project Editor: Karen Leet
Production Coordinator: Sandra Woods
Art & Design Coordinator: Carol Keohane

COPYRIGHT © 1998
By Delmar Publishers
a division of International Thomson Publishing Company

I(T)P®   The ITP logo is a trademark under license

Printed in the United States of America

For more information, contact:

Delmar Publishers
3 Columbia Circle Drive, Box 15015
Albany, New York 12212-5015

International Thomson Publishing
Berkshire House
168-173 High Holborn
London, WC1V7AA
England

Thomas Nelson Australia
102 Dodds Street
South Melbourne 3205
Victoria, Australia

Nelson Canada
1120 Birchmont Road
Scarborough, Ontario
M1K 5G4, Canada

International Thomson Editores
Campos Eliseos 385, Piso 7
Col Polanco
11560 Mexico, DF Mexico

International Thomson Publishing GmbH
Konigswinterer Str. 418
53227 Bonn
Germany

International Thomson Publishing Asia
221 Henderson Bldg. #05-10
Singapore 0315

International Thomson Publishing Japan
Hirakawacho Kyowa Building, 3F
2-2-1 Hirakawacho
Chiyoda-ku, Tokyo 102
Japan

1 2 3 4 5 6 7 8 9 10 XXX 03 02 01 00 99 98 97

Library of Congress Cataloging-in-Publication Data

Herr, Judy.
    Creative resources of art, brushes, buildings . . . / Judy Herr, Yvonne
Libby.
       p.   cm.
    ISBN 0-7668-0015-6
    1. Education, Preschool—Curricula. 2. Creative activities and
seat work.   3. Unit method of teaching.   4. Art—Study and teaching—
Activity programs.   I. Libby, Yvonne. II. Title.
LB1140.4.H477   1998
372.21—dc21   97-11206
                                                         CIP

CONTENTS

PREFACE

While reviewing early childhood curriculum resources, it becomes apparent that few books are available using a thematic or unit approach for teaching young children. As a result, our university students, colleagues, and alumni convinced us of the importance of such a book. Likewise, they convinced us of the contribution the book could make to early childhood teachers and, subsequently, to the lives of young children.

Before preparing the manuscript, we surveyed hundreds of child care, preschool, and kindergarten teachers. Specifically, we wanted them to share their curriculum problems and concerns. Our response has been to design and write a reference book tailored to their teaching needs using a thematic approach. Each theme or unit contains a flowchart, theme goals, concepts for the children to learn, theme-related vocabulary words, music, fingerplays, science, dramatic play, creative art experiences, sensory, mathematics, cooking experiences, and resources. Additionally, creative ideas for designing child-involvement bulletin boards and parent letters have been included. These resources were identified, by the teachers included in our survey, as being critical components that have been lacking in other curriculum guides.

In addition to the themes included in this book, others can be found in *Creative Resources of Colors, Food, Plants, and Occupations* and *Creative Resources of Birds, Animals, Seasons, and Holidays*. More can and should be developed for teaching young children. The authors, however, wish to caution the readers that it is the teacher's responsibility to select, plan, and introduce developmentally appropriate themes and learning experiences for his group of children. Specifically, the teacher must tailor the curriculum to meet the individual needs of the children. Consequently, we encourage all teachers to carefully select, adapt, or change any of the activities in this book to meet the needs, abilities, and interests of their group of children to ensure developmental appropriateness. A handy reference for checking developmental norms is included on pages xiii and xiv.

As you use this guide, you will note that some themes readily lend themselves to particular curriculum areas. As a result, the number of activities listed under each curriculum area will vary from theme to theme.

The detailed Introduction that follows is designed to help teachers use the book most effectively. It includes:

1. a discussion on how to develop the curriculum using a thematic approach;
2. a list of possible themes;
3. suggestions for writing parent letters;
4. methods for constructing and evaluating creative involvement bulletin boards; and
5. criteria for selecting children's books.

This book would not have been possible without the constant encouragement provided by our families, the laboratory teachers in the Child and Family Study Center, and the faculty, students, and alumni of the University of Wisconsin-Stout. Our thanks to all of these people and especially to Carla Ahmann, Susan Babler, Mary Babula, Terry Bloomberg, Margaret Braun, Renee Bruce, Anne Budde, Michelle Case, Jill Church, Bruce Cunningham, Jeanette Daines, Carol Davenport, Jill Davis, Mary DeJardin, Linda DeMoe, Rita Devery, Donna Dixon, Esther Fahm, Lisa Fuerst, Shirley Gebhart, Judy Gifford, Nancy Graese, Barbara Grundleger, Betty Herman, Patti Herman, John Herr, Mark Herr, Joan Herwig, Carol Hillmer, Priscilla Huffman, Margy Ingram, Paula Iverson, Angela Kaiser, Elizabeth (Betz) Kaster, Trudy King, Leslie Koepke, Beth Libby, Janet Maffet, Marian Marion, Janet Massa, Nancy McCarthy, Julie Meyers, Betty Misselt, Teresa Mitchell, Kathy Mueller, LaVonne Mueller, Robin Muza, Paula Noll, Sue Paulson, Mary Pugmire, Kelli Railton, Lori Register, Peg Saienga, Kathy Schaeffer, Mary Selkey, Cheryl Smith, Sue Smith, Amy Sprengler, Karen Stephens, Barbara Suihkonen, Judy Teske, Penny Warner, Connie Weber, Ed Wenzell, Mary Eileen Zenk, and Karen Zimmerman. We are also grateful to our reviewers: Gerri A. Carey, McLennan Community College, Waco, TX; Billie Coffman, PA College of Technology, Williamsport, PA; Ione Garcia, IL State University, Normal, IL; Ned Sauls, Wayne Community College, Goldsboro, NC; and Becky Wyatt, Murray State College, Tishomingo, OK. Finally, our special thanks to two individuals whose assistance made this book possible. Jay Whitney, our editor from Delmar, provided continous encouragement, support, and creative suggestions. Also, special thanks to Robin Muza, our typist and research assistant.

INTRODUCTION

The purpose of this introduction is to explain the process involved in curriculum planning for young children using the thematic or unit approach. To support each theme, planning and construction ideas are included for bulletin boards, parent letters, and a wide variety of classroom learning experiences.

Curriculum Planning

As you use this guide, remember that children learn best when they can control and act upon their environment. Many opportunities should be available for seeing, touching, tasting, learning, and self-expression. Children need hands-on activities and choices. To construct knowledge, children need to actively manipulate their environment. To provide these opportunities, the teacher's primary role is to set the stage by offering many experiences that stimulate the children's senses and curiosity; children learn by doing and play is their work. As a result, it is the authors' intention that this book will be used as a resource. Specifically, the ideas in this book should help you to enrich, organize, and structure the children's environment, providing them an opportunity to make choices among a wide variety of activities that stimulate their natural curiosity. Knowledge of child development and curriculum must be interwoven. To illustrate, play in the classroom should be child-centered and self-initiated. To provide an environment that promotes these types of play, it is the teacher's role to provide unstructured time, space, and materials. Using a theme approach to plan curriculum is one way to ensure that a wide variety of classroom experiences are provided. Successful early child-hood programs provide interesting, challenging, and engaging environments. Children need to learn to think, reason, and become decision makers.

It is important that all curricula be adapted to match the developmental needs of children at a particular age or stage of development. An activity that is appropriate for one group of children may be inappropriate for another. To develop an appropriate curriculum, knowledge of the typical development of children is needed. For this reason, the section following this Introduction contains such information. Review these developmental norms before selecting a theme or specific activities.

Theme Planning

A developmentally appropriate curriculum for young children integrates the children's needs, interests, and abilities and focuses on the whole child. Cognitive, social, emotional, and physical development are all included. Before planning curriculum, observe the children's development. Record notes of what you see. At the same time, note the children's interests and listen carefully. Children's conversations provide clues; this information is vital in theme selection. After this, review your observations by discussing them with other staff members. An appropriate curriculum for young children cannot be planned without understanding their development and interests.

There are many methods for planning a curriculum other than using themes. In fact, you may prefer not to use a theme during parts of the year. If this is your choice, you may wish to use the book as a source of ideas, integrating activities and experiences from a variety of the themes outlined in the book.

Planning a curriculum using a theme approach involves several steps. The first step involves selecting a theme that is appropriate for the developmental level and interests of your group of children. Themes based on the children's interests provide intrinsic motivation for exploration and learning. Meaningful experiences are more easily comprehended and remembered. Moreover, curiosity, enjoyment of participation, and self-direction are heightened. After selecting a theme, the next step is developing a flowchart. From the flowchart, goals, conceptual understandings, and vocabulary words can easily be extracted. The final step in curriculum planning is selecting activities based upon the children's stages of development and available resources. While doing this, refer to pages xiii and xiv, Developmental Benchmarks, to review development charcteristics for children of different ages.

To help you understand the theme approach to curriculum development, each step of the process will be discussed. Included are assessing the children's needs, and developing flowcharts, theme goals, concepts, vocabulary, and activities. In addition, suggestions are given for writing parent letters, designing bulletin boards, and selecting children's books.

Assessment

Assessment is important for planning curriculum, identifying children with special needs, and communicating a child's progress to parents. Assessment needs to be a continuous process. It involves a process of observing children during activities throughout the day, recording their behaviors, and documenting their work. Assessment involves records and descriptions of what you observe while the behavior is occurring. Logs and journals can be developed. The developmental norms that follow this Introduction can be used as a checklist of behavior. You can create a profile of the children's individualized progress in developing skills. Your observations should tell what the children like, don't like, have discovered, know, and want to learn.

Samples of the children's work in an individual portfolio collection should be maintained. A portfolio documents the children's progress, achievements, and efforts. Included should be samples of the children's paintings, drawings, storytelling experiences, oral and written language. Thus, the portfolio will include products and evidence of the children's accomplishments.

By reviewing the assessment materials you can deduce the children's developmental needs and interests. This information will be important in selecting a theme that interests the children and in selecting developmentally appropriate learning experiences.

Flowcharts/Webbings. The flowchart is a simple way to record all possible subconcepts that relate to the major concept or theme. To illustrate, plan a theme on apples. In the center of a piece of paper, write the word "apple." Then using an encyclopedia as a resource, record the subconcepts that

are related. Include origin, parts, colors, tastes, sizes, textures, food preparation, and nutrition. The flowchart on page ix includes these concepts. In addition, under each subconcept, list content that could be included. For example, apples may be colored green, yellow, or red. By using a thematic approach, we teach children the way environments and humans interconnect. This process helps children make sense out of the human experience.

Theme Goals. Once you have prepared a flowchart webbing, abstracting the theme goals is a simple process. Begin by reviewing the chart. Notice the subheadings listed. For the unit on apples, the subheadings include: foods, parts, forms, and colors. Writing each of these subheadings as a goal is the next step of the process.

Since there were four subheadings, each of these can be included as a goal. In some cases, subheadings may be combined. For example, note the fourth goal listed. It combines several subheadings.

Through participation in the experiences provided by using apples as a curriculum theme, the children may learn:

1. Parts of an apple.
2. Preparation of apples for eating.
3. Apple tastes.
4. Textures, sizes, and colors of apples.
5. The origin of an apple.

Concepts. The concepts must be related to the goal; however, they are more specific. To write the concepts, study the goals. Then prepare sentences that are written in a simple form that children can understand. Examples of concepts for a unit on apples may include:

1. An apple is a fruit.
2. An apple has five parts: seed, core, meat, skin, and stem.
3. Apples grow on trees.
4. A group of apple trees is called an orchard.
5. Bread, pies, puddings, applesauce, dumplings, butter, and jellies can be prepared from apples.
6. Some apples are sweet; others are sour.
7. Apples can be colored green, yellow, or red.
8. Apples can be large or small.
9. Apples can be hard or soft.
10. Apples can be eaten raw.
11. Seeds from an apple can grow into a tree.

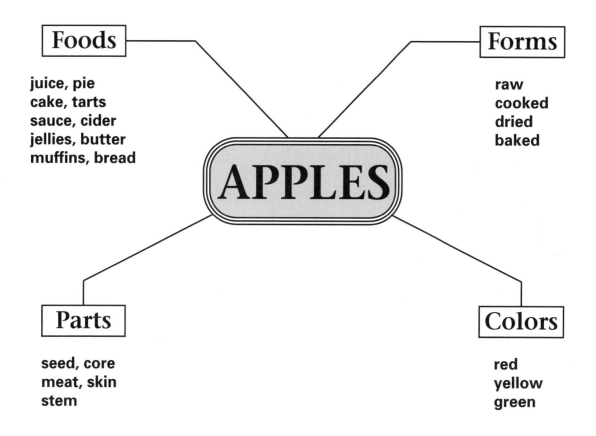

Foods

juice, pie
cake, tarts
sauce, cider
jellies, butter
muffins, bread

Forms

raw
cooked
dried
baked

APPLES

Parts

seed, core
meat, skin
stem

Colors

red
yellow
green

Vocabulary. The vocabulary should include new words that you want to informally introduce to the children. Vocabulary words need to be tailored to meet the specific needs of your group of children. The number of vocabulary words will vary, depending upon the theme and the developmental level of the children. For example, it might be assumed that the children know the word sweet, but not tart. So, the definition of the word tart is included. Collectively, the following words could be introduced in this unit: apple, texture, core, blossom, and apple butter. Definitions for these words could include:

1. apple—a fruit that is grown on a tree.
2. texture—how something feels.
3. core—the part of the apple that contains the seeds.
4. apple blossom—a flower on the apple tree.
5. apple butter—a spread for bread made from apples.

Activities. Now that you have learned how to develop goals related to a theme using a flowchart, you will need to learn how to select developmentally appropriate activities. You will find that many theme goals can be accomplished by additions to the environment, bulletin boards, field trips, and stories or resource people at group time. Your major role as an adult, or teacher, is that of a facilitator, planning and preparing the environment to stimulate the child's natural curiosity.

To begin this process, review each goal and determine how it can be introduced in the classroom. For example, if you were going to develop a theme on apples, review the goals. A bulletin board or game could introduce the three colors of apples. The children could also learn these colors through cooking experiences. The third vehicle for teaching the colors of apples would be placing the three colors of apples on a science table.

The five parts of an apple could also be introduced through participation in a tasting or cooking experience, bulletin board, or even discussion on a field trip or at the snack table. Always remember that children need to observe and manipulate the concrete object while engaged in child-initiated or child-directed play that is teacher supported. For that reason, fresh apples could be cut horizontally and placed on the science table with a magnifying glass. Likewise, simultaneously, apple seeds and paper could be

available on the art table to construct a collage. Always remember that the best activities for young children are hands-on and open-ended. That is: focus on the process, rather than the product. Children need to learn to think, reason, and become problem solvers. As a teacher, you should take the ideas in this book and use and adapt them for planning and preparing the environment. Always remember that successful early childhood programs provide interesting, challenging, and engaging environments.

Parent Letters

Communication between the child's home and school is important. It builds mutual understanding and cooperation. With the efficiency of modern technology, parent letters are a form of written communication that can be shared on a weekly basis. The most interesting parent letters are written in the active voice. They state that the subject did something. To illustrate, "Mark played with blocks and read books today."

When writing the parent letter, consider the parent's educational level. Then write the letter in a clear, friendly, concise style. To do this, eliminate all words that are not needed. Limit the length of the letter to a page or two. To assist you with the process, an example of a parent letter is included for each theme.

Parent letters can be divided into three sections. Included should be a general introduction, school activities, and home activities. One way to begin the letter is by introducing new children or staff, or sharing something that happened the previous week. After this, introduce the theme for the coming week by explaining why it was chosen.

The second section of the parent letter could include some of the goals and special activities for the theme. Share with the parents all of the interesting things you will be doing at school throughout the week. By having this information, parents can initiate verbal interaction with their child.

The third section of the parent letter should be related to home activities. Suggest developmentally appropriate activities that the parents can provide in the home. These activities may or may not relate to the theme. Include the words of new songs and fingerplays. This section can also be used to provide parenting information such as the developmental value of specific activities for young children.

Bulletin Boards

Bulletin boards add color, decoration, and interest to the classroom. They also communicate what is happening in the classroom to parents and other visitors. The most effective bulletin boards involve the child. That is, the child will manipulate some pieces of the board. As a result, they are called involvement bulletin boards. Through the concrete experience of interacting with the bulletin board materials, children learn a variety of concepts and skills. Included may be size, shape, color, visual discrimination, eye-hand coordination, etc.

Carefully study the bulletin boards included for each theme in this book. They are simple, containing a replica of objects from the child's immediate environment. Each bulletin board has a purpose. It teaches a skill or concept.

As you prepare the bulletin boards provided in this book, you will become more creative. Gradually, you will combine ideas from several bulletin boards as you develop new themes for curriculum.

An opaque projector is a useful tool for individuals who feel uncomfortable with their drawing skills. Using the opaque projector, you can enlarge images from storybooks, coloring books, greeting cards, wrapping paper, etc. To do this, simply place the image to be copied in the projector. Then tape paper or tagboard on the wall. Turn on the projector. Using a pencil, color marker or crayon, trace the outline of the image onto the paper or tagboard.

Another useful tool for preparing bulletin boards is the overhead projector. Place a clear sheet of acetate on the picture desired for enlargement. This may include figures from a coloring book or storybook. Trace around the image using a washable marker designed for tranparencies. Project the image onto a wall and follow the same procedures as with the opaque projector.

To make your bulletin board pieces more durable, laminate them. If your center does not have a laminating machine, use clear contact paper. This process works just as well, but it can be more expensive.

Finally, the materials you choose to use on a bulletin board should be safe and durable. Careful attention should be given when selecting attachments. For two-, three- and four-year-old children, adhesive velcro and staples are preferred attachments. Push pins may be used with older children under careful supervision.

Selecting Books

Books for young children need to be selected with care. Before selecting books, once again, refer to the section following this Introduction and review the typical development for your group of young children. This information can provide a framework for selecting appropriate books.

There are some general guidelines for selecting books. First, children enjoy books that relate to their experiences. They also enjoy action. The words written in the book should be simple, descriptive, and within the child's understanding. The pictures should be large, colorful, and closely represent the actions.

A book that is good for one group of children may be inappropriate for another. You must know the child or group of children for whom the story is being selected. Consider their interests, attention span, and developmental level.

Developmental considerations are important. Two-year-olds enjoy stories about the things they do, know, and enjoy. Commonplace adventure is a preference for three-year-olds. They like to listen to things that could happen to them, including stories about community helpers. Four-year-old children are not as self-centered. These children do not have to be part of every situation that they hear about. Many are ready for short and simple fantasy stories. Five-year-olds like stories that add to their knowledge; that is, books that contain new information.

Curriculum Planning Guide

We hope you find this book to be a valuable guide in planning curriculum. The ideas should help you build curriculum based upon the children's natural interests. The book should also give you ideas so that your program will provide a wide variety of choices for children.

In planning a developmentally valid curriculum, consult the Index by Subject. It has been prepared to allow you easy selection from all the themes. So pick and choose and make it your own! The Index is arranged by subject as follows:

—Art
—Cooking
—Dramatic Play
—Features (by Theme)
—Field Trips/Resource People
—Fingerplays
—Group Time
—Large Muscle
—Math
—Rain Day
—Science
—Sensory
—Songs

Other Sources

Early childhood educators should refer to other Delmar publications when developing appropriate curriculum, including:

1. Oppenheim, Carol. *Science is Fun!*
2. Green, Moira. *474 Science Activities for Young Children.*
3. Herr, Judy and Libby, Yvonne. *Creative Resources of Birds, Animals, Seasons, and Holidays.*
4. Herr, Judy and Libby, Yvonne. *Creative Resources of Colors, Food, Plants, and Occupations.*
5. Green, Moira. *Themes With a Difference: 228 New Activities for Young Children.*
6. Green, Moira. Not! *The Same Old Activities for Early Childhood.*
7. Mayesky, Mary. *Creative Activities for Young Children* (5th ed.).
8. Pica, Rae. *Experiences in Movement with Music, Activities, and Theory.*
9. American Chemical Society and American Institute of Physics. *The Best of WonderScience.*
10. Wheeler, Ron. *Creative Resources for Elementary Classrooms and School Age Programs.*
11. Bouza-Koster, Joan. *Growing Artists.*
12. Herr, Judy and Libby, Yvonne. *Creative Resources for the Early Childhood Classroom* (2nd ed.).

DEVELOPMENTAL BENCHMARKS

Ages	Fine Motor Skills	Gross Motor Skills
Two Year Olds	Turns pages in a book singly Imitates drawing a circle, vertical, and horizontal lines Fingers work together to scoop up small objects Constructs simple two- and three-piece puzzles Enjoys short, simple fingerplay games Strings large beads on shoelace Builds tower of up to eight blocks	Kicks large ball Jumps in place Runs without falling Throws ball without falling Walks up and down stairs alone Marches to music Tends to use legs and arms as pairs Uses whole arm usually to paint or color
Three Year Olds	Cuts paper Builds tower of nine small blocks Pastes using a finger Pours from a pitcher Copies a circle from a drawing Draws a straight line Uses fingers to pick up small objects Draws a person with three parts Strings beads and can arrange by color and shape Uses a knife to spread at meal or snack time	Catches ball with arms extended forward Throws ball underhand Completes forward somersault Walks up stairs with alternating feet Rides a tricycle skillfully Runs, walks, jumps, and gallops to music Throws ball without losing balance Hops on one foot
Four Year Olds	Buttons or unbuttons buttons Cuts on a line with scissors Completes a six- to eight-piece puzzle Copies a "t" Buckles a belt Zips separated fasteners Adds five parts to an incomplete man	Walks up and down stairs one foot per step Skips on one foot Rides a bicycle with training wheels
Five Year Olds	Uses a knife Copies most letters Traces objects Draws crude objects Colors within lines Copies square, triangle, and diamond shape Models objects from clay Laces shoes	Tries roller and ice skating Catches ball with hands Jumps from heights Jumps rope Walks on stilts Skips Climbs fences
Six Year Olds	Ties bows Hand preference established Reverses letters while printing Paints houses, trees, flowers, and clouds	Plays hopscotch Enjoys ball play Plays simple, organized games such as "hide-and-seek"

DEVELOPMENTAL BENCHMARKS

Ages	Emotional and Social Skills	Intellectual Skills
Two Year Olds	Takes toys away from others Plays near other children, but not cooperatively Unable to share toys Acts negatively at times Seeks teacher's attention Expresses fear of the dark Observes others to see how they do things	Talks mostly to himself Uses "me" instead of proper name Enjoys showing and naming objects Uses a two- to three-hundred word vocabulary Speaks in phrases or three-word sentences Answers yes/no questions Follows two-step commands Constructs negative sentences (no truck, no truck) Uses modifiers such as some, all, one Understands concepts big and little Uses such adjectives as red, old, and pretty
Three Year Olds	Plays in groups of two or three children Begins to take turns Sharing becomes evident with friends Enjoys independence by doing things for themselves, i.e., "Let me do it" or "I can do it." Yells "stop it" at times as opposed to striking another child	Asks "how," "what," "when," and "why" questions Uses verb such as "could," "needs," "might," and "help" Uses adverbs such as "how about" and "maybe" Understands the pronouns you and they Understands "smaller" and "larger" Answers "how" questions appropriately Loves words such as "secret," "surprise," and "different" Uses words to define space such as "back," "up," "outside," "in front of," "in back of," "over," "next to"
Four Year Olds	Loves other children and having a "friend" Bases friendships on shared activities Seeks approval of friends Plays with small groups of children Delights in humorous stories Shows more interest in other children than adults Excludes children he does not like Loves to whisper and tell secrets	Experiences trouble telling the difference between reality and fantasy Exaggerates in practicing new words Loves silly language and to repeat new silly words Vocabulary of 1200 to 1500 words Begins to identify letters in his name Begins to appreciate bugs, trees, flowers, and birds Learns simple card games and dominoes Develops an awareness of "bad" and "good"
Five Year Olds	Prefers playing in small groups Prefers friends of same sex and age Protects younger children Plays well with older siblings Washes hands before meals Respects other people's property Becomes competitive Develops sense of fairness Verbally expresses anger	Names the days of the week Writes numbers from one to ten Retells main details of stories Recognizes the cause and effect of actions Uses a vocabulary of 2000 or more words Tells original stories Follows three-step command Recognizes square and rectangle shape Recognizes numerals 1-5
Six Year Olds	Prefers friends of the same sex Engages in cooperative play involving role assignments Enjoys being praised and complimented Enjoys "show and tell" time May be argumentative Competitive and wants to win	Identifies penny, nickel, and dime Counts ten objects Completes a 15-piece puzzle Acts out stories Plays Chinese checkers and dominoes Recognizes letters and words in books Identifies right from left hand Prints numbers from 1-20 Repeats an 8-10 word sentence Counts numbers to 30

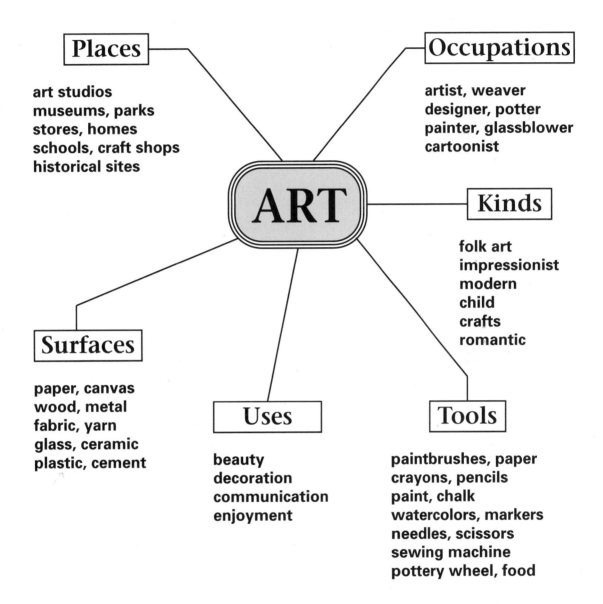

Places

art studios
museums, parks
stores, homes
schools, craft shops
historical sites

Occupations

artist, weaver
designer, potter
painter, glassblower
cartoonist

ART

Kinds

folk art
impressionist
modern
child
crafts
romantic

Surfaces

paper, canvas
wood, metal
fabric, yarn
glass, ceramic
plastic, cement

Uses

beauty
decoration
communication
enjoyment

Tools

paintbrushes, paper
crayons, pencils
paint, chalk
watercolors, markers
needles, scissors
sewing machine
pottery wheel, food

Theme Goals:

Through participating in the experiences provided by this theme, the children may learn:

1. The uses of art.

2. Places where works of art can be found.

3. Art tools.

4. Surfaces used for art.

5. Occupations associated with art.

Concepts for the Children to Learn:

1. Art is an expression of feelings and thoughts.

2. Brushes, paints, pencils, felt-tip markers, crayons, chalk, and paper are all art tools.

3. An artist uses art tools to make designs, pictures, or sculptures.

4. Art is a form of communication.

5. A museum has art objects.

6. An art gallery sells art objects.

7. Paper, canvas, and wood can all be painted.

8. We are all artists.

9. Artists create for many reasons—personal enjoyment, gift giving, and career.

Vocabulary:

1. **art**—a form of beauty.

2. **crayon**—an art tool made of wax.

3. **paint**—a colored liquid used for decoration.

4. **paintbrush**—a tool for applying paint.

5. **chalk**—a soft stone used for writing or drawing.

6. **artist**—a person who creates art.

7. **gallery**—a place to display works of art.

Bulletin Board

The purpose of this bulletin board is to reinforce color matching skills. Construct a crayon match bulletin board by drawing 16 crayons on white tagboard. Divide the crayons into pairs. Color each pair of crayons a different color. Include the colors pink, red, blue, yellow, purple, orange, brown, and green. Hang one from each pair on the top of the bulletin board and attach a corresponding colored string from the crayons. Hang the second set of crayons on the lower end of the bulletin board. A push pin can be added to the bottom set of crayons and the children can match the top crayons to their corresponding match on the bottom of the bulletin board.

Adjust the bulletin board to match the developmental needs and level of the children. For younger children, use fewer color choices. Let the children use the bulletin board during self-directed and self-initiated play periods. Repetition of this activity is important for assimilation providing it is child-initiated.

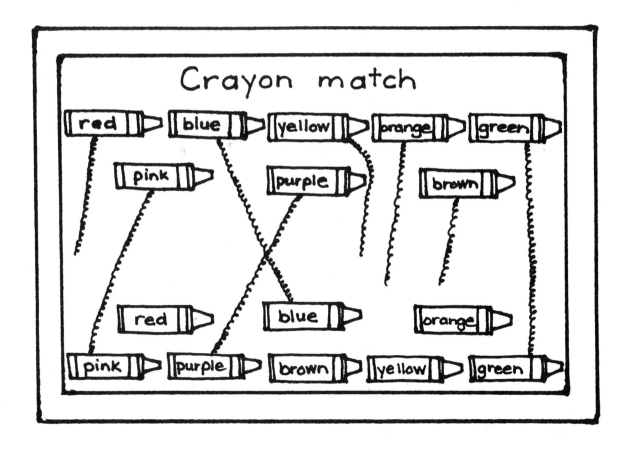

Parent Letter

Dear Parents,

Art is an expressive and aesthetic activity. It is also a curriculum theme that children always enjoy. During our focus on art, the children will be exploring many different types of art tools and supplies. They will also learn where works of art can be found. Moreover, the art work that they create will be displayed in an outdoor art gallery. You are invited to browse when you pick your child up from the center.

At School

Some of the artistic experiences planned include:

- creating chalk murals on the sidewalk.
- staging an art gallery in the dramatic play area.
- visiting on Tuesday with Bob Jones, a tour guide at the city museum. Mr. Jones will be sharing several art objects with us in our classroom.
- sorting art tools.
- participating in a wide variety of art activities.

At Home:

You can introduce the concepts of this unit into your home by collecting art tools and exploring them together. A fun art idea is to paint on paper using kitchen tools as applicators. Forks, potato mashers, and slotted spoons all work well for this activity. Through this and other art activities your child will discover interesting and creative ways to use materials. Art also provides opportunities to experiment with color.

Have fun looking at art with your child!

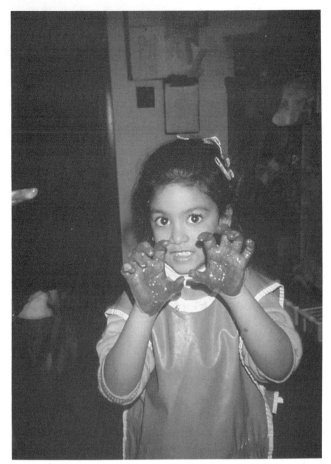

Through art, children can experience new outlets for self-expression.

Music:

"Let's Pretend"
(Sing to the tune of "Here We Are Together")

Let's pretend that we are artists,
are artists, are artists.
Let's pretend that we are artists
How happy we'll be.
We'll paint with our brushes,
and draw with our crayons.
Let's pretend that we are artists
How happy we'll be.

Fingerplays:

CLAY

I stretch it.
(pulling motion)

I pound it.
(pounding motion)
I make it firm.
(pushing motion)
I roll it.
(rolling motion)
I pinch it.
(pinching motion)
I make a worm.
(wiggling motion)

PAINTING

Hands are blue.
(look at outstretched hands)
Hands are green.
Fingers are red,
In between.
(wiggle fingers)
Paint on my face.
(touch face)
Paint on my smock.
(touch smock)
Paint on my shoes.
(touch shoes)
Paint on my socks.
(touch socks)

Social Studies:

The Feel of Color

This activity can be introduced at large group time. Begin by collecting colored construction paper. Individually hold each color up and ask the children how that particular color makes them feel. Adjectives that may be used include: hot, cold, cheerful, warm, sad, tired, happy, clean.

Group Time (games, language):

Toward the end of the unit, collect all art projects and display them in an art gallery at your center. The children can help hang their own projects and decide where to have the gallery. If weather permits, the art gallery can be set up on the playground using low clothes-lines and easels to display the art. If weather does not permit, a gallery can be set up in the classroom or center lobby, using walls and tables to display the art.

Cooking:

GRAHAM CRACKER TREAT

Give each child a graham cracker, honey, and a brush to spread the honey. Top with grated cheese, raisins, or coconut.

COOKIE DECORATING

Sugar cookies can be purchased commercially or baked and decorated. Recipes for the cookies and frosting are as follows:

1. **Drop Sugar Cookies**

   2 eggs
   2/3 cup vegetable oil
   2 teaspoons vanilla
   3/4 cup sugar
   2 cups flour
   2 teaspoons baking powder
   1/2 teaspoon salt

   Beat eggs with fork. Stir in oil and vanilla. Blend in sugar until mixture thickens. Add flour, baking powder, and salt. Mix well. Drop dough by teaspoons about 2 inches apart on an ungreased baking sheet. Flatten with the bottom of a plastic glass dipped in sugar. Bake 8 to 10 minutes or until delicate brown. Remove from baking sheet immediately. Makes about 4 dozen cookies that are 2 1/2 inches in diameter.

2. **Favorite Icing**

   1 cup sifted confectioner's sugar
   1/4 teaspoon salt
   1/2 teaspoon vanilla
   1 tablespoon water
   food coloring

   Blend salt, sugar, and vanilla. Add enough water to make frosting easy to spread. Tint with food coloring. Allow children to spread on cookie with spatula or paintbrush.

Science:

1. **Art Tools**

   A variety of art tools can be placed on the science table. Included may be brushes, pencils, felt-tip markers, crayons, and chalk. The children can observe, smell, and feel the difference in the tools.

2. **Charcoal**

   Place charcoal pieces and magnifying glasses on the science table.

3. **Rock Writing**

   Provide the children with a variety of soft rocks. The children can experiment drawing on the sidewalks with them.

Dramatic Play:

1. **Artist**

   Smocks, easels, and paint tables can be placed in the dramatic play area. The children can use the materials to pretend they are artists.

2. **Art Gallery**

   Mount pictures from magazines on sheets of tagboard. Let the children hang the pictures around the classroom. A cash register and play money for buying and selling the paintings can extend the play.

Arts and Crafts:

1. **Frames**

   During the course of this unit, the children can frame, with your assistance, their works of art by mounting them on sheets of colored tagboard and trimming it to a frame-like border. Older children may be able to do this unassisted. Display the works of art in the lobby, classroom—or outdoors, if weather permits.

2. Experimenting

In a unit on art, many kinds of art media need to be explored. Include the following art experiences:

- markers (both jumbo and skinny)
- chalk (both wet and dry)
- charcoal
- pencils (both colored and lead)
- crayons (jumbo, regular-sized, and shavings)
- paint (watercolors, tempera, fingerpaint)
- paper (colored construction, white, typing, tissue, newsprint, fingerpaint, tagboard)
- other (tin foil, cotton, glitter, glue and paste, lace, scraps, crepe paper, bags, waxed paper, yarn, and string)
- tools for painting (marbles, string, fingers, brushes of all sizes, straws, sponges)
- playdough and clay
- printing tools (stamps and ink pads, kitchen tools, sponges, potatoes, apples, and carrot ends)
- seeds

Sensory:

Additions to the Sensory Table

1. Goop

Mix together food coloring, 1 cup cornstarch, and 1 cup water in the sensory table. If a larger quantity is desired, double or triple the recipe.

2. Silly Putty

Mix food coloring, 1 cup liquid starch, and 2 cups of glue together. Stir constantly until the ingredients are well mixed. Add more starch as needed.

3. Wet Sand and Sand Mold Containers

Large Muscle:

1. Sidewalk Chalk

Washable colored chalk can be provided for the children to use outside on the sidewalk. After the activity the designs can be removed with a hose. The children may even enjoy using scrub brushes to remove the design.

2. Painting

Provide large paintbrushes and buckets of water for the children to paint the sidewalks, walls, and fences surrounding your center or school.

3. Foot Art

Prepare a thick tempera paint and pour a small amount in a shallow pan. Roll out long sheets of paper. The children can take off their shoes and socks, step into the tempera paint, and walk or dance across the sheets of paper. Provide buckets with soapy water and towels at the end of the paper for the children to wash their feet. Dry the foot paintings and send them home with the children.

Field Trips/Resource People:

1. Museum

Take a field trip to a museum, if one is available. Observe art objects. Point out and discuss color and form.

2. Art Store

Take a walk to a nearby art store. Observe the many kinds of pencils, markers, crayons, paints, and other art supplies that are available.

3. Resource People

Invite the following people to show the children their artwork.

- painter
- potter
- weaver
- glass blower
- sculptor

Math:

1. Counting Cans

Counting cans for this unit can be made from empty soup cans with filed edges. On each can write a numeral. The number prepared will depend upon the developmental needs of the children. Then provide an equal number of the following objects: pencils, pens, markers, paintbrushes, crayons, chalk sticks, sponges, etc. The object is for the children to relate the number of objects to numerals on the can.

2. **Measuring Art Tools**

Art tools come in all different lengths. Provide a variety of art tools and rulers, or a tape measure that has been taped to the table. The children can measure the objects to find which one is the longest. Make a chart showing the longest tool and continuing to the shortest.

3. **Sorting Art Supplies**

A large ice cream pail can be used to hold pencils, pens, markers, crayons, glue bottles, etc., that can be sorted into shoeboxes.

PAINTING SURFACES

There are many types of interesting surfaces that children can successfully use for painting. The list of possibilities are only limited by one's imagination. Included are:

construction paper	shelf paper	mirror
newsprint (plain/printed)	paper table cloths	plexiglass
tissue paper	paper place mats	paper bags
tracing paper	waxed paper	cookie sheets
tin foil	boxes	meat trays—plastic,
clear/colored acetate	leather scrap	cardboard, styrofoam
wood	sand paper	table surfaces
cardboard	paper toweling	

Multimedia:

The following resources can be found in educational catalogs:

1. Tsuroka, Linda, & Pliskin, Jacqueline. *Color a Song* [record].

2. Jenkins, Ella. *I Know the Colors in the Rainbow* [record].

3. *There's Music in the Colors* [record]. Kimbo Records.

4. *Fisher Price Picture Dictionary* [IBM software, PK–1]. Gametek.

Books:

The following books can be used to complement this theme:

1. Chevalier, Christa. (1982). *Spence Makes Circles*. Niles, IL: Albert Whitman and Co.

2. Williams, Vera B. (1986). *Cherries and Cherry Pits*. New York: Scholastic.

3. Tripp, Valerie. (1987). *The Penguin's Paint*. Chicago: Children's Press.

4. Kellogg, S. (1982). *Mystery of Stolen Blue Paint*. New York: Dial.

5. Moon, Marjorie (Ed.). (1988). *A Is For Art*. Milwaukee, WI: Author.

6. Reese, Bob. (1992). *Art*. Chicago: Children's Press.

7. Locker, Thomas. (1989). *The Young Artist*. New York: Dial Books for Young Readers.

8. Mayhew, James. (1989). *Katie's Picture Show*. New York: Bantam Books.

9. Carle, Eric. (1992). *The Art of Eric Carle*. Saxonville, MA: Picture Book Studio.

10. Venezia, Mike. (1988). *Van Gogh*. Chicago: Children's Press.

11. Venezia, Mike. (1991). *Michelangelo*. Chicago: Children's Press.

12. Turner, Robyn M. (1991). *Georgia O'Keefe*. New York: Little, Brown & Co.

13. dePaola, Tomie. (1988). *The Legend of the Indian Paintbrush*. New York: Putnam.

14. dePaola, Tomie. (1989). *The Art Lesson*. New York: Putnam.

15. Winter, Jeanette. (1991). *Diego*. New York: Knopf.

16. Alcorn, Johnny. (1991). *Rembrandt's Beret or the Painter's Crown*. New York: Tambourine Books.

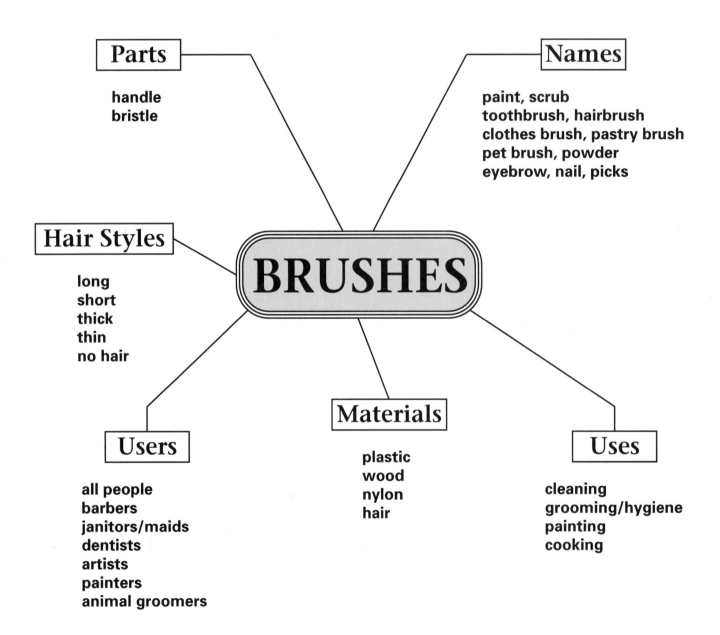

Parts

handle
bristle

Names

paint, scrub
toothbrush, hairbrush
clothes brush, pastry brush
pet brush, powder
eyebrow, nail, picks

Hair Styles

long
short
thick
thin
no hair

BRUSHES

Materials

plastic
wood
nylon
hair

Users

all people
barbers
janitors/maids
dentists
artists
painters
animal groomers

Uses

cleaning
grooming/hygiene
painting
cooking

Theme Goals:

Through participating in the experiences provided by this theme, the children may learn:

1. Parts of a brush.

2. Kinds of brushes.

3. Uses of brushes.

4. Materials used to make brushes.

5. Community helpers who need brushes for their work.

Concepts for the Children to Learn:

1. A brush is a tool.

2. Brushes come in many sizes.

3. Brushes have handles.

4. Some brushes are used in cleaning our home.

5. Toothbrushes help clean our teeth.

6. Hairbrushes are used for grooming.

7. A pastry brush is used for cooking.

8. Brushes can be made of plastic, wood, or nylon.

9. Some people use brushes while working.

Vocabulary:

1. **brush**—a tool made of bristles or wires attached to a handle.

2. **bristle**—a short, stiff hair or thread-like object.

3. **handle**—the part of a brush that is held.

4. **groom**—to clean.

5. **powder brush**—a brush that is used to apply facial powder.

6. **toothbrush**—a small brush used to clean teeth.

7. **vegetable brush**—a stiff brush used to clean vegetables.

8. **dog brush**—a brush used to clean a dog's hair.

Bulletin Board

The purpose of this bulletin board is to promote the development of color identification and matching skills. Construct and paint palette and brushes out of tagboard. Use a different colored marker to draw paint spots on each palette and to "paint" the bristles of each brush. Laminate all the pieces. Attach the palette to the bulletin board. Map tacks, putty, or velcro may be used to place the brushes next to the corresponding color of paint palette.

Parent Letter

Dear Parents,

Did you ever stop to think about the number and types of brushes we use in a day? Brushes will be the next subject that we will explore. Each one has a different function and helps us do a different job. Through the activities related to the theme, the children will become aware of the many types and uses of brushes. In addition, they will be exposed to materials used in constructing brushes.

At School

Some of the learning experiences this week will include:
- setting up a hair stylist shop in the dramatic play area (and discussing different hair styles and colors).
- "painting" outside with buckets of water and brushes.
- observing teeth being cleaned with electric and hand-held brushes as we visit Dr. Smith's dental office on Thursday morning.
- painting with a variety of brushes at the easel each day.

At Home

With your child, go through your home and locate brushes. Examples include: toothbrushes, hairbrushes, paintbrushes, fingernail polish brushes, pastry brushes, and makeup brushes. Compare and sort the various brushes. This will help your child discriminate among weights, colors, sizes, textures, and shapes. The brushes can also be counted to determine which room contains the most and which the least number of brushes, which will promote the understanding of number concepts.

Paint a picture with your child today!

Painting with water-soluble paints on pavement is a creative activity.

Music:

"Using Brushes"
(Sing to the tune of "Mulberry Bush")

This is the way we brush our teeth,
brush our teeth, brush our teeth.
This is the way we brush our teeth
So early in the morning.

Variations:
• This is the way we brush our hair....
• This is the way we polish our nails....
• This is the way we paint the house....

Act out each verse, and allow the children to make up more verses.

Fingerplays:

BRUSHES IN MY HOME

These brushes in my home
Are simply everywhere.
I use them for my teeth each day,
   (brushing teeth motion)
And also for my hair.
   (hair brushing motion)

We use them in the kitchen sink
   (scrubbing motion)
And in the toilet bowls
   (scrubbing motion)
For putting polish on my shoes
   (touch shoes and rub)
And to waterproof the soles.

Brushes are used to polish the floors
   (polishing motions)
And also paint the wall,
   (painting motion)
To clean the charcoal barbecue,
   (brushing motion)
It's hard to name them all.

MY TOOTHBRUSH

I have a little toothbrush.
   (use pointer for toothbrush)
I hold it very tightly.
   (make tight fist)
I brush my teeth each morning
   (pretend to brush teeth)
And then again at night.

SHINY SHOES

First I loosen mud and dirt,
My shoes I then rub clean.
For shoes in such a dreadful sight,
Never should be seen.

I spread the polish on the shoes.
And then I let it dry.
I brush the shoes until they shine.
And sparkle in my eye.

Science:

1. **Identifying Brushes**

   Inside the feely box, place various small brushes. The children can reach into the box, feel the object, and try to identify it by name.

2. **Exploring Bristles**

   Add to the science table a variety of brushes and magnifying glasses. Allow the children to observe the bristles up close, noting similarities and differences.

Dramatic Play:

1. **Hair Stylist**

   Collect hairspray bottles, brushes, empty shampoo bottles, chairs, mirrors, hair dryers, and curling irons, and place in the dramatic play area. Cut the cords off the electrical appliances.

2. **Water Painting**

   Outdoors provide children with buckets of water and house paintbrushes. They can pretend to "paint" the building, sidewalks, equipment, and fence.

3. **Shining Shoes**

   In the dramatic play area place clear shoe polish, shoes, brushes, and shining cloths for the children to use to polish.

Arts and Crafts:

1. **Brush Painting**

   Place various brushes such as hair, makeup, toothbrushes, and clothes brushes on a table in the art area. In addition, thin tempera paint and paper should be provided. Let the children explore the painting process with a variety of brushes.

2. **Easel Ideas**

   Each day change the type of brushes the children can use while painting at the easel.

Variations may include: sponge brushes, discarded toothbrushes, nail polish brushes, vegetable brushes, and makeup brushes.

3. **Box House Painting**

   Place a large cardboard box outside. To decorate it provide smocks, house painting brushes, and tempera paint for the children.

Large Muscle:

Sidewalk Brushing

Place buckets of water and paintbrushes for use outdoors on sidewalks, fences, and buildings.

Field Trips/Resource People:

1. **The Street Sweeper**

   Contact the city maintenance department. Invite them to clean the street in front of the center or school for the children to observe.

2. **Artist's Studio**

   Visit a local artist's studio. Observe the various brushes used.

3. **Dentist's Office**

   Visit a dentist's office. Ask the dentist to demonstrate and explain the use of various brushes.

4. **Animal Groomer**

   Invite an animal groomer to school. Ask the groomer to show the equipment, emphasizing the importance of brushes.

Math:

1. **Sequencing**

   Collect various-sized paintbrushes. Encourage the children to sequence them by height and width.

2. Weighing Brushes

Place a balance scale and several brushes in the math area. Encourage the children to weigh and balance the brushes.

3. Toothbrush Counting

Collect toothbrushes and cans. Label each can with a numeral. The children can place the corresponding number of brushes into each labeled can. If desired, the toothbrushes can be constructed out of tagboard.

Social Studies:

1. Brushes Chart

Design a "Brushes in our Classroom" chart. Encourage the children to find all that are used in the classroom.

2. Helper Chart

Design a helper chart. Include tasks such as sweeping floors, cleaning paintbrushes, putting brushes, and brooms away. This chart can encourage the children to use brushes every day in the classroom.

Group Time (games, language):

1. Brush Hunt

Hide several brushes in the classroom. Have one child search for the brushes. When he gets close to them, clap loudly. When he is further away, clap quietly.

2. Brush of the Day

At group time each day introduce a new brush. Discuss the shape, color, materials, and uses. Then allow the children to use the brush in the classroom during self-selected play period.

Cooking:

1. Cleaning Vegetables

Place several washtubs filled with water in the cooking area. Then provide children with fresh carrots and brushes. Encourage the children to clean the carrots using a vegetable brush. The carrots can be used to make carrot cake, muffins, or can be added to soup.

2. Pretzels

1 1/2 cups warm water
1 envelope yeast
4 cups flour
1 teaspoon salt
1 tablespoon sugar
1 egg
coarse salt (optional)

Mix water, yeast, sugar. Let stand for 5 minutes. Place salt and flour in a bowl. Add the yeast and stir to prepare dough mixture. Shape the dough. Beat egg and apply the egg glaze with a pastry brush. Sprinkle with salt if desired. Bake at 425 degrees for approximately 12 minutes.

PAINT APPLICATORS

There are many ways to apply paint. The size and shape of the following applicators produce unique results. While some are recycleable, others are disposable.

Recycleable Examples

paintbrushes, varying sizes and widths
whisk brooms
fingers and hands
tongue depressors or popsicle sticks
potato mashers
forks and spoons
toothbrushes
aerosol can lids
cookie cutters

spray bottles
string/yarn
roll-on deodorant bottles
squeeze bottles (plastic ketchup containers)
marbles and beads
styrofoam shapes
sponges
feet
spools
rollers

Disposable Applicators to Use with Paint

twigs and sticks
string/yarn
feathers
pinecones
rocks
cloth
cardboard tubes
straws
leaves
cotton balls
cotton swabs

Books:

The following books can be used to complement the theme:

1. Lillegard, Dee. (1987). *I Can Be a Beautician*. Chicago: Children's Press.

2. Tripp, Valerie. (1987). *The Penguins Paint*. Chicago: Children's Press.

3. dePaola, Tomie. (1988). *The Legend of the Indian Paintbrush*. New York: G. P. Putnam.

4. Hoban, Tara. (1987). *Dots, Spots, Speckles, & Stripes*. New York: Greenwillow.

5. Small, David. (1985). *Imogene's Antlers*. New York: Crown.

6. Testa, Fulvio. (1986). *If You Take a Paintbrush: A Book of Colors*. New York: Dial Books.

7. Quinlan, Patricia. (1992). *Brush Them Bright*. New York: Walt Disney Publishing.

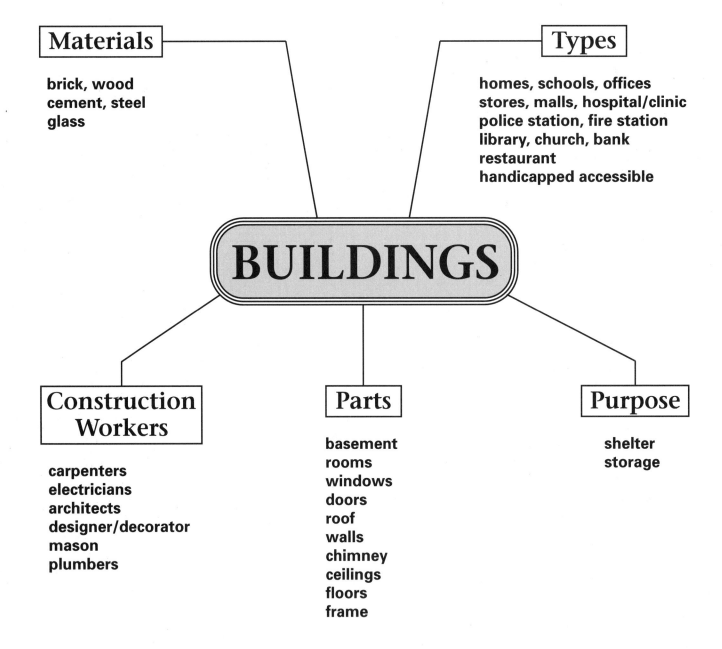

Materials

brick, wood
cement, steel
glass

Types

homes, schools, offices
stores, malls, hospital/clinic
police station, fire station
library, church, bank
restaurant
handicapped accessible

BUILDINGS

Construction Workers

carpenters
electricians
architects
designer/decorator
mason
plumbers

Parts

basement
rooms
windows
doors
roof
walls
chimney
ceilings
floors
frame

Purpose

shelter
storage

Theme Goals:

Through participating in the experiences provided by this theme, the children may learn:

1. Types of buildings.

2. Purposes of buildings.

3. Materials used to make buildings.

4. Parts of a building.

Concepts for the Children to Learn:

1. There are many types of buildings: homes, offices, stores, hospitals, malls, etc.

2. Buildings can be made of brick, wood, cement, steel, and glass.

3. Many workers help construct buildings: architects, carpenters, electricians, plumbers, and masons.

4. Buildings can be used for shelter and storage.

5. Most buildings have a roof, walls, windows, and a floor.

Vocabulary:

1. **building**—a structure.

2. **mall**—a building containing many stores.

3. **skyscraper**—a very tall building.

4. **carpenter**—a person who builds.

5. **electrician**—a person who wires a building for light, heat, and cooking.

6. **architect**—a person who designs a building.

7. **room**—a part of a building set off by walls.

8. **ceiling**—the top "wall" of a room.

9. **roof**—the top covering of a building.

Bulletin Board

The purpose of this bulletin board is to develop awareness of size as well as visual discrimination skills. Construct house shapes out of tagboard ranging in size from small to large. Color the shapes and laminate. Punch a hole in the top of each house. Trace each house shape on black construction paper and cut out. Hang the shadow pieces on the bulletin board with a push pin inserted in the top of each. During self-directed and self-initiated play, the children match each colored house to the corresponding shadow piece by hanging it on the push pin.

Parent Letter

Dear Parents,

Your home, the library, our school...these are all buildings with which your child is familiar. Buildings will be our next theme. Discoveries will be made regarding different kinds and parts of buildings, materials used to make buildings, and the people who construct buildings.

At School

A sampling of the learning experiences include:

- building with various materials—such as boxes and milk cartons.
- working at the woodworking bench to practice hammering, drilling, and sawing.
- weighing and balancing bricks.
- taking a walk to a construction site.

At Home

You can reinforce building concepts on your way to and from school by pointing out any buildings of interest, such as the fire station, police station, hospital, library, shopping mall, and restaurants. Your children are naturally curious about why and how things happen. If you pass any construction sites, point out the materials and equipment used, as well as the jobs of the workers on the sites. This will help your child develop vocabulary and language skills. Concepts of time can also be fostered if you are able to visit the construction site over an extended period of time. You and your child will be able to keep track of progress in the development of the building.

Enjoy your child as you reinforce concepts related to buildings.

Together we will build a big house.

Music:

"Go In and Out the Window"

Form a circle with the children and hold hands. While holding hands have the children raise their arms up to form windows. Let each child have a turn weaving in and out the windows. Use the following chant as you play.

_____ goes in and out the windows,
In and out the windows,
In and out the windows.
_____ goes in and out the windows,
As we did before.

Fill in child's name in the _____.

Fingerplays:

THE CARPENTER'S TOOLS

The carpenter's hammer goes rap, rap, rap
    (make hammering motion with fist)
And his saw goes see, saw, see.
    (make sawing motion with arm and hand)
He planes and hammers and saws
    (make motions for each)
While he builds a building for me.
    (point to yourself)

CARPENTER

This is the way he saws the wood
    (make sawing motion)
Sawing, sawing, sawing.

This is the way he nails a nail
    (make hammering motion)
Nailing, nailing, nailing.

This is the way he paints a building
    (make brushing motion)
Painting, painting, painting.

MY HOUSE

I'm going to build a little house.
    (draw house with fingers by outlining in the air)
With windows big and bright,
    (spread out arms)
With chimney tall and curling smoke
    (show tall chimney with hands)
Drifting out of sight.
    (shade eyes with hands to look)
In winter when the snowflakes fall
    (use fingers to make the motion of snow falling downward)
Or when I hear a storm,
    (place hand to ear)
I'll go sit in my little house
    (draw house again)
Where I'll be snug and warm.
    (hug self)

22

Science:

1. **Building Materials**

   Collect materials such as wood, brick, cement, metal, and magnifying glasses and place on the science table. Encourage the children to observe the various materials up close.

2. **Mixing Cement**

   Make cement using a small amount of cement and water. Mix materials together in a large plastic ice cream bucket. Allow the children to help. The children can also observe and feel the wet cement.

3. **Building Tools**

   Collect and place various tools such as a hammer, level, wedge, and screwdriver on the science table for the children to examine. Discuss each tool and demonstrate how it is used. Then place the tools in the woodworking area. Provide wood and styrofoam so that the children are encouraged to use the tools as a self-selected activity with close adult supervision.

Dramatic Play:

1. **Library**

   Rearrange the dramatic play area to resemble a library. Include books, library cards, book markers, tables, and chairs for the children's use.

2. **Buildings**

   Collect large cardboard boxes from an appliance dealer. The children can construct their own buildings and paint them with tempera paint.

3. **Construction Site**

   Place cardboard boxes, blocks, plastic pipes, wheelbarrows, hard hats, paper, and pencils in the dramatic play area to represent a construction site.

Arts and Crafts:

1. **Our Home**

   Provide paper, crayons, and markers for each child to draw his home. Collect all of the drawings and place them in mural fashion on a large piece of paper to create a town. To extend this activity, have the children also draw buildings in the town to extend the mural. (This activity may be limited to kindergarten children or children who have reached the representational stage of art development.)

2. **Blueprints**

   Blueprint paper, pencils, and markers should be placed in the art area. The children will enjoy marking on it. Older children may also enjoy using rulers and straight edges.

3. **Building Shapes**

   Cut out building shapes from easel paper. Place at the easel, allowing children to paint their buildings.

4. **Building Collages**

   Collect magazines with pictures of houses. Encourage children to cut or tear out pictures of buildings. The pictures can be glued on paper to create a mural.

5. **Creating Structures**

   Save half-pint milk cartons. Rinse well and allow the children to paint, color, and decorate the cartons to look like buildings.

Sensory:

1. **Wet Sand**

   Fill the sensory table with sand and add water. Provide cups, square plastic containers, bowls, etc., for children to create molds with the sand.

2. **Wood Shavings**

   Place wood shavings in the sensory table.

- electrician
- architect
- decorator/designer
- plumber

Large Muscle:

Workbench

Call attention during group time to the wood-working bench explaining the activities that can occur there. Try to encourage the children to practice pounding nails, sawing, drilling, etc., during self-initiated play.

Field Trips/Resource People:

1. **Building Site**

   Visit a local building site if available. Observe and discuss the people who are working, how buildings look, and safety. Take pictures. When the pictures are developed, post them in the classroom.

2. **Neighborhood Walk**

   Take a walk around the neighborhood. Observe the various kinds of buildings. Talk about the different sizes and colors of the buildings.

3. **Library**

   Visit a library. Observe how books are stored. Read the children a story while there. If possible, allow the children to check out books.

4. **Browsing at the Mall**

   Visit the shopping mall. Talk about the mall being a large building that houses a variety of stores. Visit a few of the stores that may be of special interest to the children. Included may be a toy store, pet store, and a sporting goods store.

5. **Resource People**

   Invite people to visit the classroom, such as:

   - construction worker
   - carpenter

Math:

1. **Weighing Bricks**

   Set out balance scale and small bricks. The children can weigh and balance the bricks.

2. **Wipe-off Windows**

   Cut out and laminate a variety of buildings with varying numbers of windows. Provide children with grease markers or watercolor markers. Encourage the children to count the number of windows of each building and print the corresponding numeral on the building. The numerals can be wiped off with a damp cloth. (This activity would be most appropriate for kindergarten children.)

3. **Blocks**

   Set out blocks of various shapes including triangles, rectangles, and squares for the children to build with.

Social Studies:

1. **Buildings in Our Town**

   Make a chart with the children's names listed vertically on the right-hand side. Across the top of the chart draw buildings or glue pictures of buildings that the children have visited. Suggestions include a theater, super-market, clinic, museum, post office, fire station, etc. At group time, ask the children what buildings they have visited. Mark the sites for each child.

2. **Unusual Buildings**

   Show pictures of unusual buildings cut from various magazines, travel guides, etc. Allow the children to use their creative thinking by asking them the use of each building. All answers and possibilities should be acknowledged.

3. **Occupation Match**

Cut out pictures of buildings and the people who work in them. Examples would include: hospital—nurse; fire station—fire fighter. Glue these pictures to tagboard and laminate. The children should be encouraged to match each worker to the appropriate building.

Group Time (games, language):

1. **Identifying Buildings**

Collect several pictures of buildings that are easily identified such as school, fire station, hospital, home. Talk about each picture. Ask, "How do you know this is a school?" Discuss the function of each building. To help the children, pictures of buildings in their community can be used.

2. **Exploring our Center**

Explore your center. Walk around the outside and observe walls, windows, roof, etc. Explore the inside also. Check out the rooms, floor, walls, ceiling, stairs... Colors, materials and size are some things you can discuss with each. Allow the children to help make an, "Our Center Has…" chart.

Cooking:

Sugar Cookies

1 1/2 cups powdered sugar
1 cup margarine or butter
1 egg
1 teaspoon vanilla
2 1/2 cups all-purpose flour
1 teaspoon baking soda
1 teaspoon cream of tartar
granulated sugar

Mix the powdered sugar, margarine, egg, and vanilla together. Stir in the flour, baking soda, and cream of tartar. Chill, to prevent sticking while rolling the dough out. Heat the oven to 375 degrees. Roll out the dough. Cut into squares, triangles, diamonds, rectangles, circles. Sprinkle with sugar. Place on a lightly greased cookie sheet. Bake until lightly brown, about 7 to 8 minutes. Give each child 3 to 5 cookies. Allow them to make buildings with their shapes before eating.

Multimedia:

The following resources can be found in educational catalogs:

1. Jenkins, Ella. *My Street Begins At My House* [record]. Kaplan.

2. *Millie's Math House*. [IBM/Mac software, PK–1]. Edmark.

Books:

The following books can be used to complement the theme:

1. Royston, Angela, & Thompson, Graham. (1990). *Monster Building Machines*. Hauppauge, NY: Barron's Educational Series.

2. Moak, Alan. (1989). *Big City ABC*. Plattsburgh, NY: Tundra.

3. Oxenbury, H. (1991). *Shopping Trip*. New York: Dial Books for Young Readers.

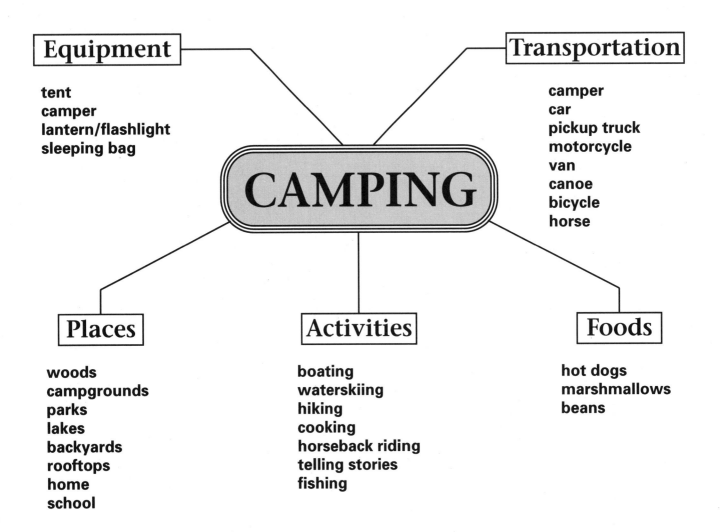

Equipment

tent
camper
lantern/flashlight
sleeping bag

Transportation

camper
car
pickup truck
motorcycle
van
canoe
bicycle
horse

CAMPING

Places

woods
campgrounds
parks
lakes
backyards
rooftops
home
school

Activities

boating
waterskiing
hiking
cooking
horseback riding
telling stories
fishing

Foods

hot dogs
marshmallows
beans

Theme Goals:

Through participating in the experiences provided by this theme, the children may learn:

1. Places where people camp.

2. Equipment used for camping.

3. Camping transportation.

4. Camping activities.

5. Foods we eat while camping.

Concepts for the Children to Learn:

1. A tent is a shelter used for camping.

2. We can camp in the woods or at a campground.

3. We can also camp in a park, at a lake, or in our backyard.

4. Hot dogs, marshmallows, and beans are all camping foods.

5. A camper can be driven or attached to the back of a car or pickup truck.

6. Lanterns and flashlights are sources of light used for camping.

7. A sleeping bag is a blanket used for camping.

8. Some people camp by a lake to water ski and go boating and fishing.

Vocabulary:

1. **backpack**—a zippered bag worn on one's back to carry objects.

2. **recreational vehicle**—a living and sleeping area on wheels.

3. **campfire**—a controlled fire that is made at a campground.

4. **campsite**—a place for tents and campers to park.

5. **camping**—living outdoors in sleeping bags, tents, cabins, or campers.

6. **woods**—an area with many trees.

7. **hiking**—taking a long walk.

8. **sleeping bag**—a zippered blanket.

9. **tent**—a movable shelter made out of material.

10. **lantern**—a covered light used for camping.

Bulletin Board

The purpose of this bulletin board is to develop recognition of colors and color words. Construct several tents out of tagboard. Make an identical set out of white tagboard. Color the first set of tents using the primary colors. Print the color names using corresponding colored markers onto the second set of tents. Laminate the materials. Staple the tents with color names to bulletin board. Punch holes in colored tents. Children can attach the tent to a push pin on the corresponding color word tent.

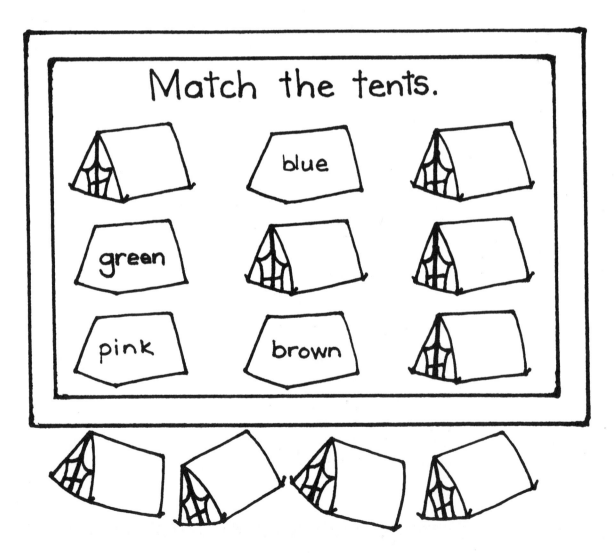

Parent Letter

Dear Parents,

With summer approaching, we will begin focusing on a fun family activity—camping! The children will become aware of items and equipment that are commonly used while camping. From listening to the children's conversations, it sounds as if many have already been camping with their family. It should be fun to hear the camping stories they will share!

At School

Some of the learning experiences planned include:

- setting up the dramatic play area with a tent, sleeping bags, and other camping items.
- singing songs around a pretend campfire.
- going on a "bear hunt" (a rhythmic chant).
- preparing foods that are eaten while camping.
- cleaning up after camping.

At Home

Help your child create a tent by draping a sheet over a table. Provide a flashlight and a blanket or sleeping bag and your child will be prepared for hours of indoor camping fun! Through dramatic play experiences children relive and clarify situations and roles. They act out how they see the world and how they view relationships among people.

If you have any photographs or slides of family camping trips, we would be delighted if you would share them with us. Contact me and we can work out a time that would be convenient for you. Thanks!

Plan a camping trip with your child today!

Having a picnic is one of the best things about camping.

Music:

1. **"A Camping We Will Go"**
   (Sing to the tune of "The Farmer and the Dell")

   A camping we will go.
   A camping we will go.
   Hi ho we're off to the woods.
   A camping we will go.

   Sue will bring the tent.
   Oh Sue will bring the tent.
   Hi ho we're off to the woods.
   A camping we will go.

   Tom will bring the food.
   Oh Tom will bring the food.
   Hi ho we're off to the woods.
   A camping we will go.

   The names in the song can be changed to
   children's names.

2. **"Two Little Black Bears"**
   (Sing to the tune of "Two Little Blackbirds")

   Two little black bears sitting on a hill
   One named Jack, one named Jill
   Run away Jack
   Run away Jill

   Come back Jack
   Come back Jill.
   Two little black bears sitting on a hill
   One named Jack, one named Jill.

3. **Campfire Songs**

   Pretend that you are sitting around a campfire.
   Explain to the children that often people sing
   their favorite songs around a campfire.
   Encourage the children to name their favorite
   songs, and then sing some of them.

Fingerplays:

BY THE CAMPFIRE

   We sat around the campfire
   On a chilly night
       (hug self)
   Telling spooky stories
   In the pale moonlight
       (look up to the sky)

   Then we added some more logs,
   To make the fire bright,
   And sang some favorite camp songs
   Together with all our might.
       (extend arms outward)
   And when the fire flickered

and embers began to form.
We snuggled in our sleeping bags
all cozy, tired, and warm.
(lie on ground, hug self)

Source: Wilmes, Liz & Dick. *Everyday Circle Times*. Building Block Publications.

FIVE LITTLE BEAR CUBS

Five little bear cubs
Eating an apple core.
One had a sore tummy
And then there were four.

Four little bear cubs
Climbing in a tree.
One fell out
And then there were three.

Three little bear cubs
Playing peek-a-boo.
One was afraid
And then there were two.

Two little bear cubs
Sitting in the sun.
One ran away
And then there was one.

One little bear cub
Sitting all alone.
He saw his mommy
And then he ran home.

Science:

1. **Scavenger Hunt**

   While outside, have the children find plants growing, insects crawling, insects flying, a plant growing on a tree, a vine, a flower, bird feathers, a root, a seed, etc.

2. **Sink/Float**

   Collect various pieces of camping equipment. Fill the water table with water and let the children test which objects sink or float. If desired make a chart.

3. **Magnifying Glasses**

   Provide magnifying glasses for looking at objects seen on a camping trip.

Dramatic Play:

1. **Camping**

   Collect various types of clothing and camping equipment and place in the dramatic play area or outdoors. Include items such as hiking boots, sweatshirts, raincoats, sleeping bags, backpacks, cooking tools, and a tent.

2. **Puppets**

   Develop a puppet corner in the dramatic play area including various animal puppets that would be seen while camping.

3. **Going Fishing**

   Set up a rocking boat or a large box in the classroom or outdoors. Prepare paper fish with paper clips attached to them. Include a fishing pole made from a wooden dowel and a long string with a magnet attached to the end.

4. **Going to the Beach**

   In the dramatic play area, set up lawn chairs, beach towels, buckets, shovels, sunglasses, etc. Weather permitting, these items could also be placed outdoors.

Arts and Crafts:

1. **Easel Ideas**

   - paint with leaves, sticks, flowers, and rocks.
   - paint with colors seen in the forest such as brown, green, yellow, and orange.
   - cut easel paper into the following shapes: tent, rabbits, chipmunks, and fish.

2. **Camping Collage**

   Collect leaves, pebbles, twigs, pine cones, etc. Provide glue and sturdy tagboard. Encourage the children to create a collage on the tagboard using the materials found while camping.

3. **Tackle Box**

   Make two holes approximately three inches apart in the center of the lid of an egg carton. To form the handle, thread a cord through the holes and tie. Paint the box. In the box, place paper clips for hooks and S-shaped styrofoam pieces for worms.

Sensory:

Sensory Table Additions

- leaves
- rocks
- pebbles
- mud and sand
- twigs
- evergreen needles and branches
- water

Large Muscle:

1. **Caves**

   Using large packing boxes or barrels placed horizontally on the playground, allow the children to pretend to be wild animals in caves.

2. **"Bear Hunt"**

   This is a chant. Prepare the children by asking them to listen and watch carefully so that they can echo back each phrase and imitate the motions as they accompany the story. Begin by patting your hands on your thighs to make foot-step sounds.

   Let's go on a bear hunt…(echo)
   We're going to find a bear…(echo)
   I've got my camera…(echo)
   Open the door, squeak…(echo)
   Walk down the walk…(echo)
   Open the gate, creak…(echo)
   Walk down the road…(echo)
   Coming to a wheat field…(echo)
   Can't go under it…(echo)
   Can't go over it…(echo)
   Have to walk through it…(echo)
       (stop patting your thighs and rub your
       hands together to make a swishing sound)
   Got through the wheat field…(echo)
   Coming to a bridge…(echo)
   Can't go under it…(echo)
   Can't go around it…(echo)

   Have to walk over it…(echo)
       (stop patting your thighs and pound your
       fists on your chest)
   Over the bridge…(echo)
   Coming to a tree…(echo)
   Can't go under it…(echo)
   Can't go around it…(echo)
   We'll have to climb it…(echo)
       (stop patting your thighs and place one fist
       on top of the other in a climbing motion)
   All the way to the top…(echo)
       (look from one side to the other)
   Do you see a bear…? (echo)
   No (shaking head)…(echo)
   We'll have to climb down…(echo)
       (place fist under fist to climb down)
   Coming to a river…(echo)
   We can't go under it…(echo)
   We can't fly over it…(echo)
   Can't go around it…(echo)
   We'll have to cross it…(echo)
   Let's get in the boat…(echo)
   And row, row, row…
       (all sing "Row, Row, Row Your Boat"
       accompanied with rowing motions)
   We got across the river…(echo)
   We're coming to a cave…(echo)
   We can't go under it…(echo)
   We can't go over it…(echo)
   Can't go around it…(echo)
   We'll have to go in it…(echo)
   Let's tip-toe
       (use fingertips to pat thighs)
       (whisper)
   It's dark inside…(echo)
   It's very dark inside…(echo)
   I can see two eyes…(echo)
   And a big furry body…(echo)
   And I feel a wet nose…(echo)
       (Yell)
   It's a BEAR….RUN….(echo)
       (patting hands very quickly)
   Run back to the river,
   Row the boat across the river,
       (rowing motion)
   Run to the tree
   Climb up and climb down
       (do climbing motion)
   Run to the bridge and cross it
       (pat chest)
   Run through the wheat field
       (swish hands together)
   Run up the road

Open the gate...it creaks,
   (open gate)
Run up the walk,
Open the door...it squeaks,
   (open door)
SLAM IT!
   (clap hands together)

Source: Wirth, Marion, Stassevitch, Verna, Shotwell, Rita, & Stemmler, Patricia. *Musical Games, Fingerplays and Rhythmic Activities for Early Childhood*. Parker Publishing Co. Inc.

Field Trips:

1. **Department Store**

   Visit a department store or a sporting goods store where camping tents and other equipment are displayed.

2. **Picnic**

   Pack a picnic lunch or snack and take it to an area campground.

3. **Camper Salesperson**

   Visit a recreational vehicle dealer and tour a large mobile home.

Math:

Camping Scavenger Hunt

   Before the children go outdoors, instruct them to find things on your playground that you would see while camping. Sort them and count them when they bring them into the classroom (five twigs, three rocks, etc.).

Social Studies:

1. **Pictures**

   Collect pictures of different campsites. Share them by displaying them in the classroom at the children's eye level.

2. **Camping Experiences**

At group time ask if any of the children have been camping. Let them tell the rest of the children what they did while they were camping. Ask where they slept, what they ate, where the bathroom was, etc.

Group Time (games, language):

1. **What's Missing**

   Have different pieces of camping equipment available to show the children. Include a canteen, portable stove, sleeping bag, cooking tools, lantern, etc. Discuss each item, and then have the children close their eyes. Take one of the objects away and then have the children guess which object is missing.

2. **Camping Safety**

   Discuss camping safety. Include these points:

   - always put out fires before going to sleep.
   - swim in safe areas and with a partner.
   - when walking, or hiking away from your campsite, always have an adult with you.
   - always wear a life jacket in the boat.

3. **Pack the Backpack**

   Bring into the classroom a large backpack. Also have many camping items available such as sweatshirts, flashlights, lanterns, foods, raincoats, etc. The teacher gives the children instructions that they are going to pretend to go on a hike to the beach. What is one thing they will need to bring along? Why? Continue until all of the children have had a chance to contribute.

Cooking:

1. **S'Mores**

   Place a large marshmallow on a square graham cracker. Next place a square of sweet chocolate on top of the marshmallow. After this, place the graham cracker on a baking sheet into a 250-degree oven for about 5 minutes or until the chocolate starts to melt. Remove the s'more and press a second graham cracker square on top of the chocolate. Let cool for a few minutes, and serve while still slightly warm.

2. **Venezuela Breakfast Cocoa**

1/4 cup water
3 tablespoons cocoa
2 tablespoons sugar
2 cups milk
1 teaspoon vanilla

1. Bring the water to a boil in a saucepan.

2. Stir in the cocoa and sugar until they are blended. Turn the heat very low.
3. Slowly pour the milk into the saucepan with the cocoa mixture. Stir steadily to keep the mixture from burning. Continue cooking the mixture over low heat for about 2 minutes. Do not let it boil or skin will form on the top.
4. When the cocoa is hot, remove it from the stove and stir in the vanilla.
5. Carefully pour the cocoa into the cups. Serve warm.

Source: Touff, Terry, & Ratner, Marilyn. (1974). *Many Hands Cooking*. New York: Thomas Y. Crowell Company.

Multimedia:

The following resources can be found in educational catalogs:

1. Wood, Lucille. *Camping in the Mountains* [record].

2. *Sounds Around* [30-minute video]. Bo Beep Production.

3. *The Backyard* [Mac software, PK–2]. Broderbund.

Books:

The following books can be used to complement the theme:

1. Henkes, Kevin. (1989). *Bailey Goes Camping*. New York: Puffin Books.

2. Rey, Margaret, & Shalleck, Alan J. (1985). *Curious George Goes Hiking*. Boston: Houghton Mifflin Company.

3. Cooke, Tom (Illus.). (1990). *Hide and Seek Camping Trip: A Sesame Street Book*. New York: Random House Books for Young Readers.

4. Allen, Julia. (1987). *My First Camping Trip*. Provo, UT: ARO Publishing Co.

5. Eeebs, Aunt. (1991). *The Happy Campers*. Houston, TX: Rivercrest Industries.

6. Hoban, Lillian. (1993). *Arthur's Campout*. New York: Harper Collins Children's Books.

7. Roche, P.K. (1991). *Webster and Arnold Go Camping*. New York: Puffin Books

8. Singer, Marilyn. (1992). *In My Tent*. New York: Macmillian Children's Book Group.

9. Ziefert, Harriet. (1990). *Harry Goes to Day Camp*. New York: Viking Children's Books.

10. Hayward, Linda. (1990). *Elmo Goes to Day Camp*. New York: Random House.

11. Hort, Lenny. (1991). *How Many Stars in the Sky?* New York: Tambourine Books.

12. Fife, Dale H. (1991). *The Empty Lot*. Boston, MA: Little Brown & Company and Sierra Club Books.

13. Jeffers, Susan. (1990). *Brother Eagle, Sister Sky*. New York: Dial.

14. Ryder, Joanne. (1991). *When the Woods Hum*. New York: Morrow Junior Books.

15. Brett, Jan. (1987). *Goldilocks and the Three Bears*. New York: G. P. Putnam.

16. Rylant, Cynthia. (1986). *Night in the Country*. New York: Bradbury Press.

17. Oughton, Jerrie. (1992). *How the Stars Fell into the Sky*. Boston, MA: Houghton Mifflin.

18. Taylor, Jane. (1992). *Twinkle, Twinkle, Little Star*. New York: Morrow.

19. Skidmore, Steve. (1991). *What a Load of Trash*. Brookfield, CA: The Millbrook Press.

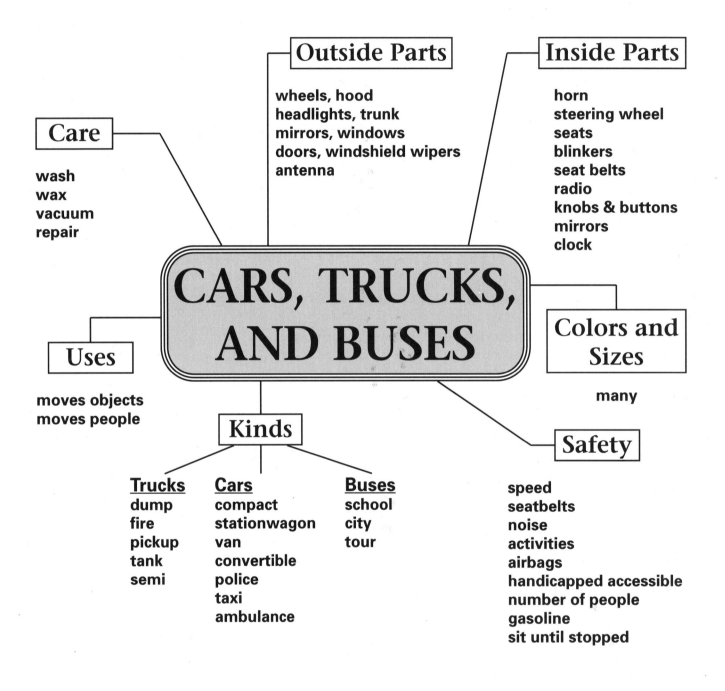

Outside Parts

wheels, hood
headlights, trunk
mirrors, windows
doors, windshield wipers
antenna

Inside Parts

horn
steering wheel
seats
blinkers
seat belts
radio
knobs & buttons
mirrors
clock

Care

wash
wax
vacuum
repair

CARS, TRUCKS, AND BUSES

Colors and Sizes

many

Uses

moves objects
moves people

Kinds

Safety

speed
seatbelts
noise
activities
airbags
handicapped accessible
number of people
gasoline
sit until stopped

Trucks
dump
fire
pickup
tank
semi

Cars
compact
stationwagon
van
convertible
police
taxi
ambulance

Buses
school
city
tour

Theme Goals:

Through participating in the experiences provided by this theme, the children may learn:

1. Kinds of cars, trucks, and buses.

2. Care of vehicles.

3. Uses of vehicles.

4. Inside and outside parts of vehicles.

5. Colors and sizes of vehicles.

Concepts for the Children to Learn:

1. There are many kinds of cars, trucks, and buses.

2. Trucks and buses are usually bigger than cars.

3. Trucks can be used to haul objects.

4. People use cars, trucks, and buses to move from place to place.

5. Compact cars are small.

6. A license is needed to drive a car, truck, or bus.

7. Cars, trucks, and buses need gas to run.

8. Gas can be obtained at a filling station.

9. Vehicles need to be vacuumed, washed, waxed, and repaired.

10. Headlights, mirrors, and wheels are parts of a car.

Vocabulary:

1. **car**—vehicle used for moving people.

2. **truck**—a wheeled vehicle used to move people and big objects.

3. **bus**—a vehicle that carries many people.

4. **driver**—operates the vehicle.

5. **passenger**—the rider.

6. **fuel**—gas, diesel, etc., used to produce power.

7. **gas**—produces power to move a vehicle.

Bulletin Board

The purpose of the bulletin board is to reinforce color recognition and matching skills, as well as develop one-to-one correspondence concepts. Construct garage shapes out of tagboard. Color each garage a different color and hang on the bulletin board. Hang a push pin in the center of each garage. Next, construct the same number of cars as garages from tagboard. Color each car a different color to correspond with the colors of the garages. Use a paper punch to make a hole in each car. The children can park each car in its corresponding colored garage.

38

Parent Letter

Dear Parents,

Cars, trucks, and buses—these are all transportation vehicles that your child sees on a regular basis. We are beginning a unit on "Cars, Trucks, and Buses." Through participating in the planned experiences, the children will learn that there are many colors, sizes, and kinds of cars, trucks, and buses. They will also become aware of the occupations associated with the vehicles including taxi drivers, bus drivers, and mechanics.

At School

Some of the activities planned for this unit include:

- painting with small cars at the art table.
- looking at many books about trucks, buses, and cars.
- setting up a gas station in the dramatic play area.
- a visit with Officer Lewis from the police department, who will show the children his squad car at 10:30 A.M. on Thursday.

At Home

You can foster the concepts of this unit at home by taking your child with you the next time you need to buy gas for your car. There are many different types of trucks and cars to observe at the filling station. Also, provide soapy water and a sponge and let your child help you wash the family car. Children enjoy taking part in grown-up activities and this helps to build a sense of responsibility and self-esteem.

Enjoy your child as you explore concepts related to cars, trucks, and buses.

Time to race cars.

Fingerplays:

OUR FAMILY CAR

This is our family car
　　(make fists as if holding a steering wheel)
The engine purrs like new.
Four wheels and a body,
　　(hold up four fingers)
It is painted blue.

Dad and Mom use it for business
　　(hold fists as if holding a steering wheel)
Or to drive us to the store.
We take it on vacation
You couldn't ask for more.
　　(shake head "no")

In the winter weather
If we should miss the bus,
　　(make sad face)
We can still get to our school,
In the family car we trust.
　　(hold fists as if holding a steering wheel)

Source: Wilmes, Liz & Dick. (1983). *Everyday Circle Times*. Building Block Publishers, Illinois.

WINDSHIELD WIPER

I'm a windshield wiper
　　(bend arm at elbow with fingers pointing up)

This is how I go
　　(move arm to left and right, pivoting at elbow)
Back and forth, back and forth
　　(continue back and forth motion)
In the rain and snow.
　　(continue back and forth motion)

HERE IS A CAR

Here is a car, shiny and bright.
　　(cup one hand and place on other palm)
This is the windshield that lets in the light.
　　(hands open, fingertips touching)
Here are wheels that go round and round.
　　(two fists)
I sit in the back seat and make not a sound.
　　(sit quietly with hands in lap)

THE CAR RIDE

(Left arm, held out bent, is road; right fist is car.)

"Vroom!" says the engine
　　(place car on left shoulder)
As the driver starts the car.
　　(shake car)

"Mmmm," say the windows
As the driver takes it far.
　　(travel over upper arm)

"Errr," say the tires
As it rounds the final bend,
   (turn at elbow, proceed over forearm)

"Ahhh," says the driver
As his trip comes to an end.
   (stop car on left flattened palm)

SCHOOL BUS

I go to the bus stop each day
   (walk one hand across table)
Where the bus comes to take us away.
   (stop, have other hand wait also)
We stand single file
   (one behind the other)
And walk down the aisle
   (step up imaginary steps onto bus)
When the bus driver talks, we obey.

Science:

1. **License Plates**

   Collect license plates from different states and different vehicles and place them on a table for the children to explore.

2. **Feely Box**

   Put transportation toys in a feely box. Include cars, trucks, and buses. Individually let the children feel inside the box and identify the type of toy.

Dramatic Play:

1. **Filling Station**

   Provide cardboard boxes for cars and hoses for the gas pumps. Also, make available play money and steering wheels.

2. **Bus**

   Set up a bus situation by lining up chairs in one or two long rows. Provide a steering wheel for the driver. A money bucket and play money can also be provided. If a steering wheel is unavailable, heavy round pizza cardboards can be used to improvise.

3. **Taxi**

   Set up two rows of chairs side by side to represent a taxi. Use a pizza cardboard, or other round object, as the steering wheel. Provide a telephone, dress-up clothes for the passengers, and a hat for the driver. A "TAXI" sign can also be placed by the chairs to invite play.

4. **Fire Truck**

   Contact the local fire chief and ask to use old hoses, fire hats, and fire fighter clothing.

Arts and Crafts:

1. **License Plate Rubbings**

   Place paper on top of a license plate. Using the side of a large crayon, rub across the top of the license plate.

2. **Car Painting**

   Provide several small plastic cars, trucks, and large sheets of white paper. Also, have available low, flat pans of thin tempera paint. Encourage the children to take the cars and trucks and roll the wheels in the paint. They can then transfer the car to their own paper and make car or truck tracks on the paper.

3. **Designing Cars**

   Provide the children with large appliance-sized cardboard boxes. To protect the floor surface, place a large sheet of plastic underneath. Provide the children with paint, markers, and collage materials to decorate the boxes as cars. When the cars dry, they can be moved into the block building, dramatic play areas, or outdoor area.

4. **Scrapbooks or Collages**

   Provide magazines for children to cut or tear out pictures of cars and trucks to make a collage or small scrapbook.

Sensory:

Sensory Table Additions

- cars and trucks with wet sand
- baby oil and water

Large Muscle:

1. **"Fill 'er Up"**

   The trikes, wagons, and scooters can be used outside on the playground. A gas pump can be constructed out of an old cardboard box with an attached hose.

2. **Car, Car, Truck**

   Play this simple variation of "Duck, Duck, Goose" by substituting the words, "Car, Car, Truck."

3. **Wash a Car**

   If possible, wash a compact-size car. Provide a hose, sponges, brushes, a bucket, and soapy water. If an actual car is not available, children can wash tricycles, bicycles, scooters, and wagons.

Field Trips/Resource People:

1. **City Bus**

   Take the children for a ride around town on a city bus. When boarding, allow each child to place his own money in the meter. Observe the length of the bus. While inside, watch how the bus driver operates the bus. Also, have a school bus driver visit and tell about the job and the importance of safety on a bus.

2. **Taxi Driver**

   Invite a taxi driver to visit and show the features of the taxi.

3. **Patrol Car**

   Invite a police officer to bring a squad car to the center. The radio, siren, and flashing lights can be demonstrated. Let the children sit in the car.

4. **Fire Truck**

   Invite a local fire fighter to bring a fire truck to the center. Let the children climb in the truck and observe the parts.

5. **Semi-truck Driver**

   Invite a semi driver to bring the truck to school. Observe the size, number of wheels, and parts of the cab. Let the children sit in the cab.

6. **Ambulance**

   Invite an ambulance driver to bring the vehicle to school. Let the children inspect the contents.

Math:

1. **Cars and Garages**

   Car garages can be constructed out of empty half-pint milk cartons. Collect and carefully wash the milk cartons. Cut out one side and write a numeral starting with one on each carton. Next, collect a corresponding number of small matchbox cars. Attach a strip of paper with a numeral from one to the appropriate number on each car's top. The children can drive each car into the garage with the corresponding numeral.

2. **License Plate Match**

   Construct two sets of identical license plates. Print a pattern of letters or numerals on each set. Mix them up. Children can try to match the pairs.

3. **Car, Truck, or Bus Sequencing**

   Cut out various-sized cars, trucks, or buses and laminate. Children can sequence them from largest to smallest and vice versa.

4. **Sorting**

Construct cars, trucks, and buses of different colors and laminate. Children can sort according to color.

Social Studies:

Discussion on Safety

Have a group discussion on safety when riding in a car. Allow children to come up with suggestions. Write them down on a chart and display in classroom during the unit. The addition of pictures or drawings would be helpful for younger children.

Group Time (games, language):

1. **Thank-You Note**

Write a thank-you note to a resource person. Allow children to dictate and sign it.

2. **Red Light, Green Light**

Select one child to pretend to be a traffic light. The traffic light places his back to children lined up at the other end of the room. When the traffic light says, "Green Light," or holds up green paper, the other children attempt to creep up on the traffic light. At any time the traffic light can say, "Red Light," or hold up a red paper and quickly turn around. Creeping children must freeze. Any child caught moving is sent back to the starting line. Play continues until one child reaches the traffic light. This child becomes the new traffic light.

Multimedia:

The following resource can be found in educational catalogs:

Car Songs [record]. Kimbo Records.

Cooking:

1. **Cracker Wheels**

For this recipe each child will need:

4 round crackers
1/2 hot dog
1/2 a slice of 4" x 4" cheese

Slice hot dogs and place on a cracker. Place cheese over the top. Place in oven at 350 degrees for 3 to 5 minutes or microwave for 30 seconds. Let cool and eat.

2. **Greek Honey Twists**

3 eggs, beaten
2 tablespoons vegetable oil
1/2 teaspoon baking powder
1/4 teaspoon salt
1 3/4 to 2 cups all-purpose flour
vegetable oil
1/4 cup honey
1 tablespoon water
ground cinnamon to taste

Mix eggs, 2 tablespoons oil, baking powder, and salt in a large bowl. Gradually stir in enough flour to make a very stiff dough. Knead 5 minutes. Roll half the dough at a time as thin as possible on well-floured surface with a stockinet-covered rolling pin. Cut into wheel shapes. Cover with damp towel to prevent drying.

Heat 2 to 3 inches of oil to 375 degrees. Fry 3 to 5 twists at a time until golden brown, turning once, about 45 seconds on each side. Drain on paper towels. Heat honey and water to boiling; boil 1 minute. Cool slightly. Drizzle over twists; sprinkle with cinnamon. Makes 32 twists.

Source: *Betty Crocker's International Cookbook*. (1980). New York: Random House.

Books:

The following books can be used to complement the theme:

1. Rockwell, Anne. (1986). *Things That Go*. New York: E. P. Dutton, Inc.

2. *Fill It Up! All About Service Stations*. (1985). New York: Thomas Y. Crowell.

3. Kunhardt, Edith T. (1985). *The Taxi Book*. New York: Golden Books.

4. Geis, Darlen. (1987). *Rattle-Rattle Dump Truck*. Los Angeles: Price/Stern/Sloan.

5. Petrie, Catherine. (1987). *Joshua James Likes Trucks*. Chicago: Children's Press.

6. Royston, Angela. (1991). *Cars*. New York: Macmillan Children's Book Group.

7. Barrett, Norman. (1990). *Custom Cars*. New York: Franklin Watts, Inc.

8. Aldog, Kurt. (1992). *Some Things Never Change*. New York: Macmillan Children's Books.

9. Greenblat, Rodney A. (1990). *Uncle Wizzmo's New Used Car*. New York: Harper Collins Children's Books.

10. Owen, Annie. (1991). *Bumper to Bumper*. New York: Alfred A. Knopf, Books for Young Readers.

11. Ross, K. K. (1990). *The Little Red Car*. New York: Random House for Young Readers.

12. Stamper, Judith. (1990). *What's It Like to Be a Bus Driver*. Mahwah, NJ: Troll Associates.

13. Grosset and Dunlop Staff. (1991). *Wheels on the Bus*. New York: Putnam Publishing Group.

14. Zelinsky, Paul O. (1990). *Wheels on the Bus: With Pictures that Move*. New York: Dutton Children's Books.

15. Herman, Gail. (1990). *Make Way for Trucks: Big Machines on Wheels*. New York: Random Books for Young Readers.

16. Strickland, Paul. (1990). *All About Trucks*. Milwaukee: Gareth Stevens, Inc.

17. Wolf, Sallie. (1992). *Peter's Trucks*. Morton Grove, IL: Albert Whitman and Co.

18. Howard, Elizabeth Fitzgerald. (1988). *The Train to Lulu's*. New York: Bradbury Press.

19. Siebert, Diane. (1990). *Train Song*. New York: Thomas Y. Crowell.

20. Robbins, Sandra. (1990). *Big Annie*. New York: Berrent Publishers.

21. Cole, Joanna. (1986). *The Magic School Bus at the Waterworks*. New York: Scholastic, Inc.

22. Schubert, Ingrid, & Schubert, Dieter. (1985). *The Magic Bubble Trip*. Brooklyn, NY: Kane/Miller.

23. Crews, Donald. (1987). *Flying*. New York: Greenwillow.

24. Pomerantz, Charlotte. (1987). *How Many Trucks Can a Tow Truck Tow?* New York: Random House.

25. Powers, Mary Ellen. (1986). *Our Teacher's in a Wheelchair*. Niles, IL: Albert Whitman.

26. Crews, Donald. (1992). *Freight Train*. New York: Morrow.

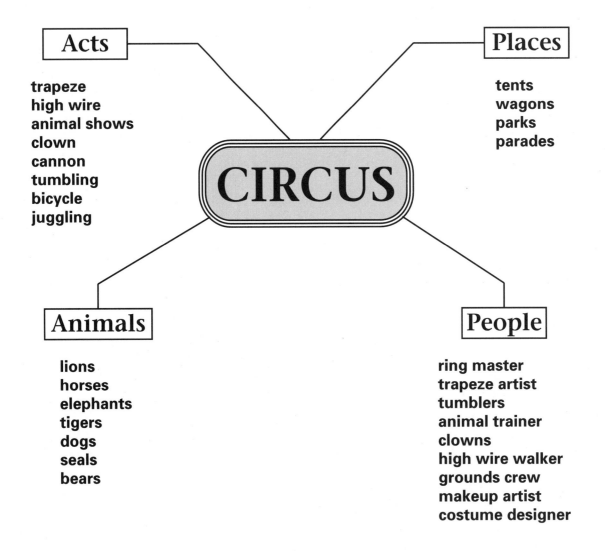

Acts

trapeze
high wire
animal shows
clown
cannon
tumbling
bicycle
juggling

Places

tents
wagons
parks
parades

CIRCUS

Animals

lions
horses
elephants
tigers
dogs
seals
bears

People

ring master
trapeze artist
tumblers
animal trainer
clowns
high wire walker
grounds crew
makeup artist
costume designer

Theme Goals:

Through participating in the experiences provided by this theme, the children may learn:

1. Different circus acts.

2. People who work for a circus.

3. Animals that perform in a circus.

4. Places to watch a circus.

Concepts for the Children to Learn:

1. The circus is fun.

2. Many adults and children enjoy the circus.

3. The circus can be performed under a big tent.

4. An animal trainer teaches animals tricks.

5. Circus shows have colorful clowns.

6. Clowns wear makeup.

7. Music is played at the circus.

8. People and animals do special tricks in the circus.

9. Many people work at the circus.

Vocabulary:

1. **circus**—traveling show with people and animals.

2. **circus parade**—a march of people and animals at the beginning of the performance.

3. **clowns**—people who wear makeup and dress in silly clothes.

4. **trapeze**—short bar used for swinging.

5. **ring master**—person in charge of the circus performance.

6. **makeup**—colored face paint.

7. **stilts**—long sticks a performer stands on to be taller.

Bulletin Board

The purpose of this bulletin board is to develop color recognition and matching skills. Construct eight clown faces with collars out of tagboard. Color each collar a different color using felt-tip markers. Hang these pieces on the bulletin board. Next, construct eight hat pieces out of tagboard. Color each one a different color, to correspond with the colors of the clowns' collars. Punch holes in the hats, and use push pins to hold the hats above the appropriate clown. The children can match the colored hats to the clown wearing the same-colored collar.

Parent Letter

Dear Parents,

We are starting a unit that is fun for everyone—the circus! It will be a very exciting unit! Developing an awareness of special people and animals enhances an appreciation of others. It also stimulates children's curiousity to learn more about other people and jobs people have. The children will be learning about the many acts and performances people and animals do at the circus.

At School

Some of the many fun and exciting things we will be doing include:

- listening to the story, *Harriet Goes to the Circus* by Betsy and Guilio Maestro.
- dressing up in clown suits and applying makeup in the dramatic play area.
- acting out a small circus of our own.
- making clown face puppets.

We will have a very special visitor come to our room on Friday—a clown! He will show us how he applies his makeup and will perform for us. You are invited to join us for the fun at 3:00 p.m. to share in this activity.

At Home

It has been said that the circus is perhaps the world's oldest form of entertainment. Pictures of circus acts drawn over 3,000 years ago have been discovered on walls of caves. Most children enjoy clowns and dressing up as clowns. Prepare clown makeup with your child by adding a few drops of food coloring to cold cream. Have your child use his fingers or a clean paintbrush to paint his face. This activity will help develop an awareness of colors, as well as help him or her realize that appearances can change but the person remains the same!

Enjoy your child!

Clowns like to make people laugh.

Music:

1. **"Circus"**
(Sing to the tune of "Did You Ever See a Lassie")

Let's pretend that we are clowns, are clowns, are clowns.
Let's pretend that we are clowns.
We'll have so much fun.
We'll put on our makeup and make people laugh hard.
Let's pretend that we are clowns.
We'll have so much fun.

Let's pretend that we are elephants, are elephants, are elephants.
Let's pretend that we are elephants.
We'll have so much fun.
We'll sway back and forth and stand on just two legs.
Let's pretend that we are elephants.
We'll have so much fun.

Let's pretend that we are on a trapeze, a trapeze, a trapeze.
Let's pretend that we are on a trapeze.
We'll have so much fun.
We'll swing high and swoop low and make people shout "oh!"
Let's pretend that we are on a trapeze.
We'll have so much fun!

2. **"The Ring Master"**
(Sing to tune of "The Farmer and the Dell")

The ring master has a circus.
The ring master has a circus.
Hi-ho the clowns are here.
The ring master has a circus.

The ring master takes a clown.
The ring master takes a clown.
Hi-ho the clowns are here.
The ring master takes a clown.

The clown takes an elephant…

Use clowns, elephants, lions, tigers, tightrope walker, trapeze artist, acrobat, etc.

Fingerplays:

GOING TO THE CIRCUS

Going to the circus to have a lot of fun.
　(hold closed fist, and raise fingers to indicate number)
The animals parading one by one.
Now they are walking 2 by 2,
A great big lion and a caribou.
Now they are walking 3 by 3,
The elephants and the chimpanzee.
Now they are walking 4 by 4,
A striped tiger and a big old bear.
Now they are walking 5 by 5,
It makes us laugh when they arrive.

ELEPHANTS

Elephants walk like this and like that.
　(sway body back and forth)
They're terribly big; they're terribly fat.
　(spread arms wide in a circular motion)
They have no hands, they have no toes,

50

And goodness gracious, what a NOSE!
(put arms together and sway for elephant nose)

FIVE LITTLE CLOWNS

Five little clowns running through the door.
(hold up one hand, put down one finger at each verse)
One fell down and then there were four.
Four little clowns in an apple tree.
One fell out and then there were three.
Three little clowns stirring up some stew.
One fell in and then there were two.
Two little clowns having lots of fun.
One ran away and then there was one.
One little clown left sitting in the sun.
He went home and then there were none!

CIRCUS CLOWN

I'd like to be a circus clown
And make a funny face,
(make a funny face)
And have all the people laugh at me
As I jump around the place.
(act silly and jump around)

THE CIRCUS IS COMING

The circus is coming hurray, hurray!
(clap hands)
The clowns are silly; see them play.
(make a face)
The animals parade one by one
(walk fingers on lap)
While clowns juggle balls for fun.
(pretend to juggle)
The lion growls; the tigers roar,
(paw in the air)
While the elephant walks on all fours.
(swing arms like an elephant trunk)
The circus is coming hurray, hurray!
(clap hands)

Source: Rountree, Barbara, et al. (1981). *Creative Teaching with Puppets*. Alabama: The Learning Line, Inc.

Science:

1. **Circus Balloons**

   Cut several pieces of tagboard into circles. If desired, cover the balloons with transparent contact or lamination paper. On each table have three cups of colored water—red, yellow, and blue—with a brush in each cup. The child can mix all or any two colors and see which colors they can create for their circus balloons.

2. **Shape the Clown**

   Cut several large outlines of clowns' heads from tagboard or construction paper and many eyes, hats, ears, noses, ruffles, and bowties. Make a large die with an ear, nose, hat, eye, ruffle, and bow tie. (One on each of the six sides.) The children can take turns rolling the die to construct their clown face. If a child rolls a die with the shape they already have, they must wait for their next turn.

   Source: *Teacher-made Games*. (1980). Missouri: Parent-Child Early Education.

3. **Seal and Ball Color/Word Match**

   Cut several seals out of different-colored tagboard. Out of the same colors cut several balls. Write the correct color on each ball. The children match each ball with the word on it to the correct seal.

4. **Sizzle Fun**

   Pour 1 inch of vinegar in a soda or catsup bottle. Put 2 teaspoons of baking soda inside a balloon. Quickly slip the open end of the balloon over the soda bottle. Watch the balloon fill with gas created by the interaction of the vinegar with the baking soda.

5. **Texture Clown**

   Construct a large clown from tagboard. Use different textured materials to create the clown's features. Make two sets. Place the extra set in a box or a bag. The children may pick a piece of textured material from the bag and match it to the identical textured piece used as a clown feature.

6. **Make Peanut Butter**

Take the shells off of fresh peanuts. Blend peanuts in a blender until smooth. Add 1 1/2 to 2 tablespoons of oil per cup of peanuts and blend well. Add 1/2 teaspoon salt per cup if desired. Spread on bread or crackers and eat for snack.

Dramatic Play:

1. **Clown Makeup**

Prepare clown makeup by mixing 1 part facial cream with 1 drop food coloring. Place clown makeup by a large mirror in the dramatic play area. The children apply makeup to their faces. Clown suits can also be provided if available.

2. **Circus**

Set up a circus in your classroom. Make a circle out of masking tape on the floor. The children can take turns performing in the ring. The addition of Hula Hoops, animal and clown costumes, tickets, and chairs would extend the children's play in this area.

3. **Animal Trainers**

Each child can bring in their favorite stuffed animals on an assigned day. The children can pretend to be animal trainers for the circus. They may select to act out different animal performances.

Arts and Crafts:

1. **Clown Stencils**

Cut several clown figures out of tagboard. Place felt-tip markers, crayons, pencils, and stencils on the art table. The children can trace the stencils.

2. **Easel Ideas**

- clown face-shaped paper
- circus tent-shaped paper

3. **Circus Wagons**

Collect old cardboard boxes and square food containers. The children can make circus wagons by decorating the boxes. When each child is through making their wagon, all of the boxes can be placed together for a circus train.

4. **Clown Face Masks**

Provide paper plates and felt-tip markers to make paper plate clown masks. Glue the plate to a tongue depressor. The children can use the masks as puppets.

5. **Playdough Animals**

Prepare playdough by combining:

2 cups flour
1 cup salt
1 cup hot water
2 tablespoons oil
4 teaspoons cream of tartar
food coloring

Mix the ingredients. Then knead the mixture until smooth. This dough may be kept in a plastic bag or covered container. If the dough becomes sticky, add additional flour.

6. **Peanut Shell Collages**

Provide peanut shells, glue, and paper for the children to create collages.

Sensory:

Provide rubber or plastic animal figurines for the children to play with in the water table.

Large Muscle:

1. **Tightrope Walker**

Provide a balance beam and a stick for the children to hold perpendicular to their bodies.

2. Dancing Elephants

Provide each child a scarf and play music. The children can pretend to be dancing elephants.

3. Bean Bag Toss

Make a large clown or other circus person or animal bean bag toss out of thick cardboard. Cut the eyes, nose, and mouth holes all large enough for the bean bags to go through. For older children, assign each hole a certain number of points and maintain a score chart or card.

4. Can Stilts

Provide large tin cans with prebored holes on sides and thick string or twine for the children to make can stilts. Once completed, the children stand on the cans and walk around the room.

5. Tightrope Transition

As a transition, place a 10-foot line of masking tape on the floor. The children can pretend to tightrope walk over to the next activity.

6. Monkey, Monkey, Clown

Play Duck, Duck, Goose but change the words to Monkey, Monkey, Clown.

These games are most appropriate for older children—four-, five-, six-, and seven-year-olds.

Field Trips/Resource People:

1. Clown Makeup

Invite a clown to demonstrate putting on makeup. Then have the clown put on a small skit and talk about the circus.

2. The Circus

If possible, go to a circus or circus parade in your area.

Math:

1. Clown Hat Match

Make sets of matching colored hats. On one set print a numeral. On the matching hats print an identical number of dots. The children match the dots to the numbers.

2. Circus Sorting

Find several pictures of symbols that represent a circus. Also include other pictures. Place all pictures in a pile. The children can sort pictures into two piles. One pile will represent circus objects.

3. Growing Chart

Make a giraffe growing chart. If desired, another animal can be substituted. Record each child's height on the chart at various times during the year.

Social Studies:

1. Circus Life

Read *You Think It's Fun to be a Clown!* by David A. Adler. When finished, discuss the lives of circus people.

2. Body Parts

Make a large clown out of tagboard. Make corresponding matching body parts such as arms, legs, ears, shoes, hands, and fingers. The children can match the parts.

Group Time (games, language):

1. Making a Clown

Give each child a paper and one crayon. Have children draw as you recite this fingerplay:

Draw a circle round and big,
Add a few hairs as a wig.
Make a circle for a nose,

Now a smile, broad and wide.
Put an ear on either side.
Add some eyes, but not a frown.
Now you have your very own clown.

This activity should only be used with older children when it is developmentally appropriate and when self-selected during small group time.

Source: Indenbaum, Valerie & Shapiro, Marcia. (1985). *The Everything Book for Teachers of Young Children*. Michigan: Partner Press.

2. Circus Pictures

Place pictures of clowns and circus things around the room at the children's eye level. Introduce the pictures at group time and discuss each picture.

3. Who Took My Nose?

Prepare red circles from construction paper. Seat the children in a circle. Give each child a red circle to tape on their nose. Then, have everyone close their eyes. Tap one child. This child should get up and go to another child and take his nose. When the child returns to his place the teacher claps her hands and all the children open their eyes. The children then try to identify the child who took the nose.

4. Clown Lotto

Adhere clown face stickers, or draw simple clown faces, on several 2-inch x 2-inch pieces of tagboard. Also, prepare lotto boards using the same stickers or drawings. To play, turn all cards face down. Children take turns choosing a card from the table and seeing if it matches a picture on their game boards.

Cooking:

1. Clown Snack

Place a pear in the middle of a plate. Sprinkle grated cheese on the pear for hair. Add raisin eyes, a cherry nose, and a raisin mouth. Finally, make a ruffle collar from a lettuce leaf.

2. Cheese Popcorn

1/4 cup butter
1/4 cup dry cheddar cheese
3 cups popped popcorn

Melt butter and grate cheese. Mix together and pour over popcorn. Stir until well coated. Salt to taste if desired.

Source: Warren, Jean. (1982). *Super Snacks*. Alderwood Manor, WA: Warren Publishing House.

Multimedia:

The following resources can be found in preschool educational catalogs:

1. Palmer, Hap. *Pretend* [record].

2. Wood, Lucille. *Animals and Circus* [record].

3. Wood, Lucille & Tanner. "Circus Parade" on *Rhythm Time* [record].

4. *Kindergarten Carnival* [record]. Melody House.

5. *Do It Yourself Kid's Circus* [record]. Kimbo.

Books:

The following books can be used to complement the theme:

1. McCully, Emily. (1992). *Mirette on the High Wire*. New York: Putnam.

2. Doty, Roy. (1991). *Wonderful Circus Parade*. New York: Simon and Schuster Trade.

3. Ehlert, Lois. (1992). *Circus*. New York: Harper Collins Children's Books.

4. Goennel, Heidi. (1992). *The Circus*. New York: William Morrow and Co.

5. DeHieronymis, Elve F. (1989). *A Night at the Circus*. New York: Barron.

6. Hill, Eric. (1986). *Spot Goes to the Circus*. New York: Putnam.

7. Moncure, Jane B. (1987). *A Color Clown Comes to Town*. Mankato, MN: Child's World.

8. Peppe, Rodney. (1985). *Circus Numbers: A Counting Book*. New York: Delacorte.

9. Peppe, Rodney. (1989). *Thumbprint Circus*. New York: Delacorte.

10. Petersham, Maud, & Petersham, Miska. (1989). *The Circus Baby*. New York: Macmillan.

11. Prelutsky, Jack. (1989). *Circus!* New York: Macmillan.

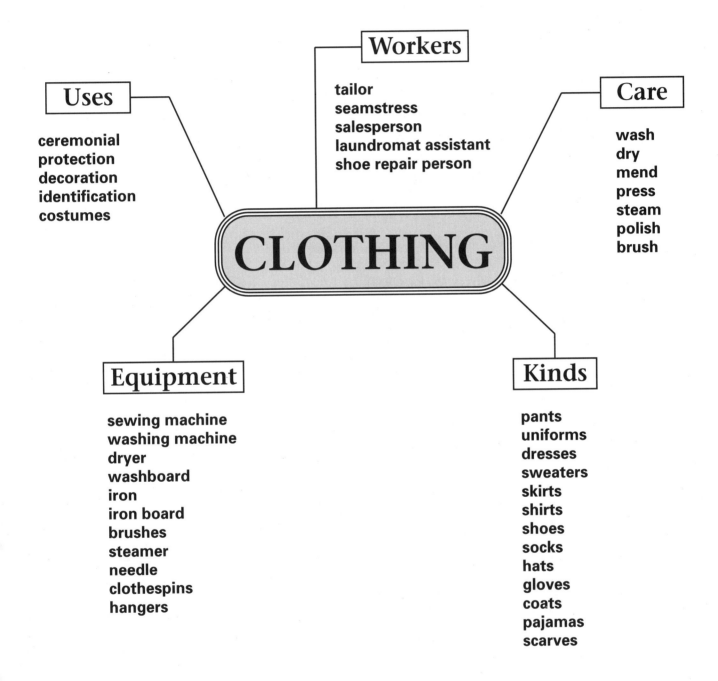

Workers

tailor
seamstress
salesperson
laundromat assistant
shoe repair person

Uses

ceremonial
protection
decoration
identification
costumes

Care

wash
dry
mend
press
steam
polish
brush

CLOTHING

Equipment

sewing machine
washing machine
dryer
washboard
iron
iron board
brushes
steamer
needle
clothespins
hangers

Kinds

pants
uniforms
dresses
sweaters
skirts
shirts
shoes
socks
hats
gloves
coats
pajamas
scarves

Theme Goals:

Through participating in the experiences provided by this theme, the children may learn:

1. Types of clothing.
2. Clothing workers.
3. Uses of clothing.
4. Care of clothing.
5. Equipment used with clothing.

Concepts for the Children to Learn:

1. Clothing is a covering for our body.
2. Pants, dresses, shirts, and sweaters are some of the clothing we wear on our bodies.
3. Shoes, socks, and boots are clothing for our feet.
4. Gloves and mittens are coverings for our hands.
5. Hats and scarves are coverings for our head.
6. Protection, decoration, and identification are uses for clothing.
7. There are many colors and sizes of clothing.
8. A tailor and a seamstress make and mend clothing.
9. Clothing needs to be cleaned.
10. Clothespins and hangers are used to hang clothes.
11. Clothes identify workers.
12. Needles, brushes, and irons are needed to care for clothing.

Vocabulary:

1. **clothing**—a covering for the body.
2. **shirt**—clothing that covers the chest and sometimes arms.
3. **shoes**—clothing for our feet.
4. **skirt**—clothing that hangs from the waist.
5. **hat**—clothing that covers our head.
6. **coat/jacket**—a piece of clothing that is often used for warmth and is worn over other clothing.
7. **clothespin**—a clip used to hang clothes on a clothesline or a hanger.
8. **washing machine**—an appliance used to clean clothes.
9. **dryer**—an appliance that dries clothes.
10. **laundromat**—a place to clean clothes.

Bulletin Board

The purpose of this bulletin board is to develop visual perception and discrimination skills. A "Sort the Clothes" bulletin board can be an addition to the clothing unit. Construct shorts and shirt pieces out of tagboard. The number used will be dependent upon the size of the bulletin board and the age of the children. Draw a pattern on a pair of shorts and the same pattern on one of the shirts. Continue, drawing a different pattern for each shorts and shirt set. Hang the shorts on the bulletin board, and hang a push pin on top of the shorts, so the children can hang the corresponding patterned shirt on top of the shorts.

Parent Letter

Dear Parents,

We will be beginning a unit on clothing. Through participating in this unit, the children will learn about many different kinds of clothing. They will also become aware of the care of clothing and purposes of clothing.

At School

Some of the learning experiences planned for this unit include:

- sorting clothes hangers by color.
- going to a laundromat in the dramatic play area.
- making newspaper skirts at the art table.
- washing doll clothes in the sensory table.

We will also be taking a walk to the Corner Laundromat on Tuesday afternoon. We will be looking at the big laundry carts, washers and dryers, and folding tables. If you would like to join us, please contact me. We will be leaving the center at 3:00 p.m.

At Home

You can foster the concepts introduced in this unit by letting your child select what he will wear to school each day. To promote independence, begin by placing your child's clothes in a low drawer allowing easy access to the clothes. To make mornings more enjoyable, encourage your child to select clothes at night that can be worn the next day. Find a location to place the clothes. Also, if your child has doll clothes, fill the kitchen sink or a tub with soapy water, and let your child wash the doll clothes. This will help your child become aware of the care of clothes.

Have fun exploring concepts related to clothing.

We take turns washing the clothes.

Fingerplay:

DRESS FOR THE WEATHER

If you go without your coat
    (put on coat)
When the wind is damp and chill,
    (hug self)
You could end up in bed, my friend,
    (shake finger)
Feverish, sneezing, and ill.
    (look sick, sneeze)
Wear your boots through snow and mud
    (put on boots)
And during a thunderstorm.
Also wear a waterproof coat and hat
    (put on coat and hat)
To keep yourself dry and warm.

Source: Cromwell, Hibner, & Faitel. (1983).
Finger Frolics. Michigan: Partner Press.

Science:

Fabric Sink and Float

Provide various kinds of clothing and fabric on the science table along with a large tub of water. The children can test the different types of clothing to see which will sink and which will float. Some clothing articles will sink while other clothing articles float until they become saturated with water. After a test has been made, the clothes can be hung to dry.

Dramatic Play:

1. **Clothing Store**

   Place dress-up clothing on hangers and a rack. A cash register, play money, bags, and small shopping carts can also be provided to extend the play.

2. **Party Clothes**

   Provide dressy clothes, jewelry, shoes, hats, and purses.

3. **Uniforms**

   Collect occupational clothing and hats, such as police officer shirts and hats, a fire fighter's hat, nurse and doctor lab coats, and artist smocks. High school athletic uniforms can also be provided. After use, store this box so the uniforms are available upon request for other units.

4. Hanging Clothes

String a low clothesline in the classroom or outdoors. Provide clothespins and doll clothes for the children to hang up.

5. Laundromat

Collect two large appliance-sized boxes. Cut a hole in the top of one to represent a washing machine, and cut a front door in the other to represent a dryer. A laundry basket, empty soap box, and play clothing may be welcome additions to extend the play.

Arts and Crafts:

1. Dress the Paper Doll

Prepare clothing to fit paper dolls out of construction paper scraps. For younger children, the dolls can be pre-cut. Older children may be able to cut their own dolls if the lines are traced on paper, and a simple pattern is provided.

2. Newspaper Skirts

Depending upon the developmental level of the children, newspaper skirts can be constructed in the classroom. Begin by stapling about 10 sheets of newspaper across at the top. Draw a bold line about two inches from the staples. Then instruct the children to vertically cut from the bottom edge of the paper, all the way up to the bold line, creating strips. String pieces can be attached by stapling to the top of both sides to enable the skirt to be tied in the back.

3. Easel Ideas

- feature clothes-shaped easel paper
- paint using tools created by attaching small sponges to a clothespin

Sensory:

1. Washing Clothes

Fill the sensory table with soapy water and let the children wash doll clothing. After being washed, the clothes can be hung on a low clothesline.

2. Add to the Sensory Table

- clothespins

Large Muscle:

1. Clothespin Drop

Collect clothespins and a series of jars with mouth openings of varying widths. The children can stand near the jar and drop the clothespins into it. To ensure success, the younger children should be guided to try the jar with the largest opening.

2. Bean Bag Toss

Bean bags can be tossed into empty laundry baskets.

3. Clothes Race

Fill bags with large-sized clothing items. Give a bag to each child. Signal the children to begin dressing up with the clothing. The object is to see how quickly they can put all of the clothes items in the bag over their own clothing. This activity is more appropriate for five-, six-, and seven-year-olds who have better large motor coordination and development.

Field Trips/Resource People:

1. Clothing Store

Visit a children's clothing store. Look at the different colors, sizes, and types of clothing.

2. Tailor/Seamstress

Invite a seamstress to visit your classroom to show the children how they make, mend, and repair clothing. The seamstress can demonstrate tools and share some of the clothing articles they have made.

3. Laundromat

Take a walk to a local laundromat. Observe the facility. Point out the sizes of the different

kinds of washing machines and dryers.
Explain the use of the laundry carts and
folding tables.

Math:

1. **Clothes Seriation**

   Provide a basketful of clothes for the children
   to line up from largest to smallest. Include
   hats, sweatshirts, shoes, and pants. Use
   clothing items whose sizes are easily
   distinguishable.

2. **Line 'em Up**

   Print numerals on clothespins. The children
   can attach the clothespins on a low clothesline
   and sequence them in numerical order.

3. **Hanger Sort**

   Colored hangers can be sorted into laundry
   baskets or on a clothesline by color.

4. **Sock Match**

   Collect many different pairs of socks. Combine
   in a laundry basket. The children can find the
   matching pairs and fold them.

Social Studies:

1. **Weather Clothing**

   Bring in examples of clothing worn in each of
   the four seasons. Provide four laundry baskets.
   Label each basket with a picture representing a
   sunny hot day, a rainy day, a cold day, and a
   fall or spring day. Then encourage the children
   to sort the clothing according to the weather
   label on the basket.

2. **Who Wears It?**

   At group time, hold up clothing items and ask
   the children who would wear it. Include baby
   clothes, sports uniforms and occupational
   clothing, ladies clothes, men's clothes, etc.

Group Time:

Look Closely

While the children are sitting on the floor in a
circle, call out the clothes items that one child
is wearing. For example, say, "I see someone
who is wearing a red shirt and pants." The
children can look around the circle and say the
name of the child who is wearing those items.

Cooking:

1. **Graham Crackers**

   Wear chef uniforms, and make your own
   graham crackers for snack.

   1/2 cup margarine
   2/3 cup brown sugar
   1/2 cup water
   2 3/4 cups graham flour
   1/2 teaspoon salt
   1/2 teaspoon baking powder
   1/8 teaspoon cinnamon

   Beat margarine and sugar till smooth and
   creamy. Add the remainder of the ingredients
   and mix well. Let the mixture sit for 30 to 45
   minutes. Sprinkle flour on a board or tabletop.
   Roll out dough to 1/8 inch thick. Cut the
   dough into squares, logs, or whatever. Place on
   an oiled cookie sheet. Bake at 350 degrees for
   20 minutes until lightly brown. This recipe
   should produce a sufficient quantity for eight
   children.

2. **Irish Gingerbread**

   1 or 2 teaspoons butter
   2 cups flour
   1 1/2 teaspoon baking soda
   1 teaspoon cinnamon
   1 teaspoon ground ginger
   3/4 teaspoon salt
   1 egg
   2 egg yolks
   1 cup molasses
   1/2 cup soft butter
   1/2 cup sugar
   1/2 cup quick-cooking oatmeal
   1 cup hot water

Preheat the oven to 350 degrees. Grease the bottom of the baking pan with 1 or 2 teaspoons of butter. Measure the flour, baking soda, cinnamon, ginger, and salt; sift them together onto a piece of waxed paper. In a mixing bowl, combine the butter with the sugar by stirring them with the mixing spoon until they are blended. Add the egg and egg yolks. With the mixing spoon, beat the mixture until it is fluffy. Stir in the molasses.

Add the sifted dry ingredients, the oatmeal, and the hot water one fourth at a time to the egg and molasses mixture, stirring after each addition. Pour the mixture into the greased pan. Bake 50 to 55 minutes. Test with a toothpick. Make gingerbread people with cookie cutters. Decorate: make clothes for the gingerbread people using coconut, nuts, raisins, etc.

Source: Touff, Terry, & Ratner, Marilyn. (1974). *Many Hands Cooking*. New York: Thomas Y. Crowell Co.

3. **Pita or Pocket Bread**

1 package of yeast
1/4 cup of lukewarm water
3 cups of flour
    (white, whole wheat, or any combination)
2 teaspoons of salt

Dissolve the yeast in the water and add the flour and salt. Stir into a rough sticky ball. Knead on a floured board or table until smooth, adding more flour, if necessary. Divide the dough into 6 balls and knead each ball until smooth and round. Flatten each ball with a rolling pin until 1/4 inch thick and about 4 to 5 inches in diameter.

Cover the dough with a clean towel and let it rise for 45 minutes. Arrange the rounds upside down on baking sheets. Bake in a 500-degree oven for 10 to 15 minutes or until brown and puffed in the center. The breads will be hard when they are removed from the oven, but will soften and flatten as they cool. When cooled, split or cut the bread carefully and fill with any combination of sandwich filling.

DRAMATIC PLAY CLOTHES

The following list contains names of clothing articles to save for use in the dramatic play area:

aprons	socks	coats
boots	purses	earmuffs
pajamas	jewelry— rings	raincoats
shirts	bracelets	snow pants
dresses	necklaces	shorts
skirts	clip-on earrings	sweatsuits
hats	shoes	suspenders
gloves/mittens	slippers	billfolds
scarves	robes	ties
leotards	slacks	belts
swimsuits	sweaters	

Multimedia:

The following resource can be found in educational catalogs:

Palmer, Hap. "What Are You Wearing?" on *Learning Basic Skills through Music* [record].

Books:

The following books can be used to complement the theme:

1. Corey, Dorothy. (1985). *New Shoes!* Niles, IL: Albert Whitman & Co.

2. Tyrrell, Anne. (1987). *Elizabeth Jane Gets Dressed*. Woodbury, NY: Barron's.

3. Daly, Niki. (1986). *Not So Fast, Songololo*. New York: Atheneum.

4. Winthrop, Elizabeth. (1986). *Shoes*. New York: Harper and Row.

5. Hill, Ari. (1986). *The Red Jacket Mix-up*. New York: Golden Press.

6. Hoban, Tara. (1987). *Dots, Spots, Speckles and Stripes*. New York: Greenwillow Books.

7. Fitz-Gerald, Christine Maloney. (1987). *I Can Be a Textile Worker*. Chicago: Children's Press.

8. Shreckhise, Roseva. (1985). *What Was It Before It Was a Sweater?* Chicago: Children's Press.

9. Flournoy, Valerie. (1985). *The Patchwork Quilt*. New York: Dial Press.

10. Oliver, Stephen. (1991). *Clothes*. New York: Random House Books for Young Readers.

11. Pluckrose, Henry. (1990). *Wear It!* New York: Franklin Watts, Inc.

12. Allen, Jonathan. (1992). *Purple Sock, Pink Sock*. New York: William Morrow and Co.

13. Gaban, Jesus. (1992). *Harry Dresses Himself*. Milwaukee: Gareth Stevens, Inc.

14. Neitzel, Shirley. (1992). *The Dress I'll Wear to the Party*. New York: Greenwillow Books.

15. Rice, Eve. (1989). *Peter's Pocket*. New York: Greenwillow Books.

16. Roy, Ron. (1991). *Whose Shoes are These?* Boston: Houghton Mifflin Co.

17. Hilton, Nettle. (1990). *The Long Red Scarf*. Minneapolis: Carolrhoda Books.

18. Blackman, Marjorie. (1992). *A New Dress for Maya*. Milwaukee: Gareth Stevens Children's Books.

19. Brett, Jan. (1989). *The Mitten*. New York: G. P. Putnam.

20. Peek, Merle. (1985). *Mary Wore Her Red Dress and Henry Wore His Green Sneakers*. New York: Clarion.

21. Borden, Louise. (1989). *Caps, Hats, Socks, and Mittens*. New York: Scholastic.

22. Carlstrom, Nancy White. (1986). *Jesse Bear, What Will You Wear?* New York: Macmillan.

23. Hest, A. (1986). *The Purple Coat*. New York: Four Winds.

24. Brown, Marc. (1989). *One, Two Buckle My Shoe*. New York: Dutton.

THEME

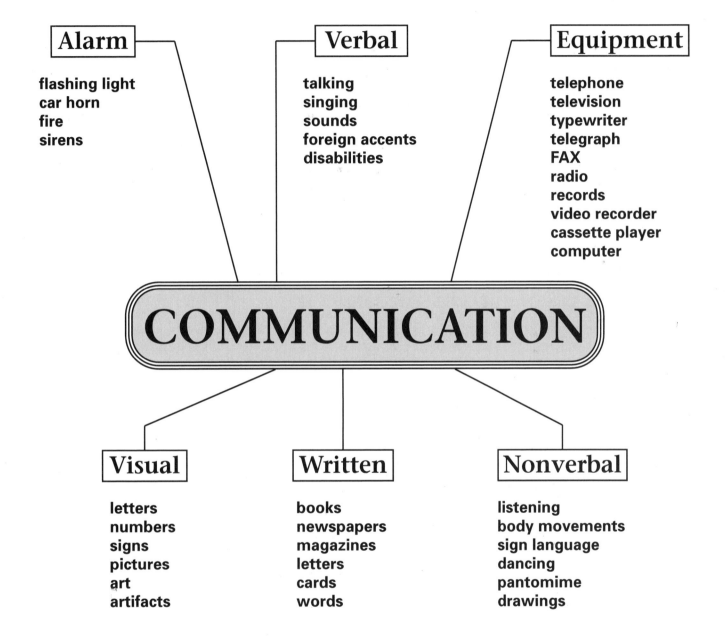

Alarm

flashing light
car horn
fire
sirens

Verbal

talking
singing
sounds
foreign accents
disabilities

Equipment

telephone
television
typewriter
telegraph
FAX
radio
records
video recorder
cassette player
computer

COMMUNICATION

Visual

letters
numbers
signs
pictures
art
artifacts

Written

books
newspapers
magazines
letters
cards
words

Nonverbal

listening
body movements
sign language
dancing
pantomime
drawings

Theme Goals:

Through participating in the experiences provided by this theme, the children may learn:

1. Visual communication skills.

2. Nonverbal communication skills.

3. Verbal communication skills.

4. Communication equipment.

Concepts for the Children to Learn:

1. Talking is a form of communication.

2. Listening is a way to communicate.

3. Our hands can communicate.

4. Our faces can communicate.

5. Sign language is a way of communication.

6. The telephone is a communication tool.

7. Letters and cards are a way of communicating.

8. Machines can transmit messages.

9. Typewriters, televisions, radios, and computers are equipment for communicating.

10. Signs are a way of communicating.

11. Books are a form of communication.

Vocabulary:

1. **communication**—sharing information.

2. **typewriter**—a machine that prints letters.

3. **newspaper**—words printed on paper.

4. **sign language**—making symbols with our hands to communicate.

5. **Braille**—a system of printing for blind people.

6. **alphabet**—letter symbols that are used to write a language.

7. **signs**—symbols.

8. **card**—a piece of folded paper with a design. Cards are sent to people on special occasions: birthdays, holidays, celebrations, or when ill.

9. **letter**—paper with a written or typed message.

Bulletin Board

The purpose of this bulletin board is to assist older children in learning their home telephone number. Construct a telephone and receiver for each child. See the illustration. Affix each child's telephone number to the telephone. Laminate this card. For younger children, receivers can be attached to the telephones but left off the hook. The children can hang up their receiver when they arrive at school. Older children can match their receiver to their number and correct themselves by the color match. Later, white receivers for each child could be used to see if they know their telephone number. Telephones can be prepared for dialing by fastening the rotary dial with a brass fastener. Then the children can practice calling home by dialing their own number.

Parent Letter

Dear Parents,

We will begin talking about communication or how we get our ideas across to others. Through this unit the children will become aware of the different ways we communicate: through our voices, letters, using hands, and our bodies. They will also become familiar with machines that are used to communicate such as the television, radio, computer, typewriter, and telephone.

At School

Some of the learning experiences planned for this unit include:

- a sign language demonstration.
- a phone booth in the dramatic play area.
- a typewriter in the writing center.
- songs and books about communication.

At Home

It is important for children to know their telephone number for safety reasons. Help your children learn your home telephone number. (This is also something we will be practicing at school.) To make practicing more fun, construct a toy telephone with your child. Two paper cups or empty tin cans and a long piece of rope, string, or yarn are needed to make a telephone. Thread the string through the two cups and tie knots on the ends. Have two people hold the cups and pull the string taut. Take turns talking and listening. The sound vibrations travel through the string—and you won't hear a busy signal!

Enjoy your children as you share concepts and experiences related to communication.

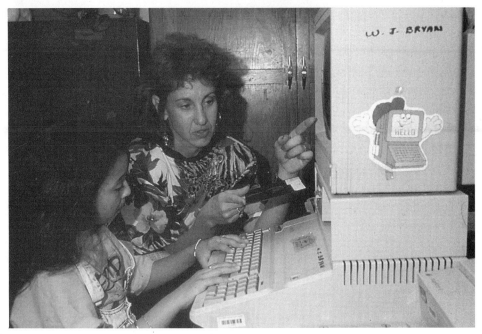

Computers are one way to communicate.

Music:

1. **"Call a Friend"**
(Sing to the tune of "Row, Row, Row Your Boat")

   Call, call, call a friend.
   Friend, I'm calling you.
   Hi, hello, how are you?
   Very good, thank you!

2. **"A Letter, A Letter"**
(Sing to the tune of "A Tisket, A Tasket")

   A letter, a letter, I can make a letter.
   I take my arms and take my legs and I can make a _____.

   Encourage the children to make letters of the alphabet with their body parts.

   Source: Wirth, Stassevitch, Shotwell, and Stemmler. *Musical Games, Fingerplays and Rhythmic Activities for Early Childhood.*

3. **"Twinkle, Twinkle Traffic Light"**
(Sing to the tune of "Twinkle, Twinkle Little Star")

   Twinkle, twinkle traffic light
   Standing on the corner bright.

   Green means go, we all know
   Yellow means wait, even if you're late.
   Red means STOP!
      (pause)
   Twinkle, twinkle traffic light
   Standing on the corner bright.

4. **"I'm a Little Mail Carrier"**
(Sing to the tune of "I'm a Little Teapot")

   I'm a little mail carrier, short and stout.
   Here is my hat, and here is my pouch.
      (point to head, point to side)
   I walk around from house to house,
   Delivering mail from my pouch.
      (pretend to take things out of a bag)

Fingerplays:

BODY TALK

   When I smile, I tell you I'm happy.
      (point at the corner of mouth)
   When I frown, I tell you that I'm sad.
      (pull down corners of mouth)
   When I raise my shoulders and tilt my head, I tell you "I don't know."
      (raise shoulders, tilt head, raise hands, shake head)

HELPFUL FRIENDS

Mail carriers carry a full pack
Of cards and letters on their backs.
   (hold both hands over one shoulder)
Step, step, step! Now ring, ring, ring!
   (step in place and pretend to ring bell)
What glad surprises do they bring?

MY HANDS

My hands can talk
In a special way.
These are some things
They help me to say.
"Hello"
   (wave)
"Come Here"
   (beckon toward self)
"It's A–OK"
   (form circle with thumb and pointer)
"Now Stop"
   (hand out–palm up)
"Look"
   (hands shading eyes)
"Listen"
   (cup hand behind ear)
Or "It's far, far away"
   (point out into the distance)
And "Glad to meet you, how are you today?"
   (shake neighbor's hand)

Science:

1. **Telephones**

   Place telephones, real or toy, in the classroom to encourage the children to talk to each other. Also, make your own telephones by using two large empty orange juice concentrate cans, removing one end for the removal of content. After washing the cans, connect with a long string. The children can pull the string taut. Then they can take turns talking and listening to each other.

2. **Sound Shakers**

   Using identical small orange juice cans, pudding cups, or empty film containers, fill pairs of the containers with different objects.

   Included may be sand, coins, rocks, rice, salt, etc. Replace the lids. Make sure to secure the lids with glue or heavy tape to avoid spilling. To make the containers self-correcting, place numbers or like colors on the bottoms of the matching containers.

3. **Feely Box**

   Prepare a feely box which includes such things as tape cassette, pen, pencil, block letters, an envelope, and anything else that is related to communication. The children can place their hand in the box and identify objects using their sense of touch.

4. **Training Telephones**

   Contact your local telephone company to borrow training telephones. Place the telephone on the science table along with a chart listing the children's telephone numbers. The children can sort, match, and classify the wires.

5. **Vibrations**

   Encourage the children to gently place their hand on the side of the piano, guitar, record player, radio, television, etc., in order to feel the vibrations. Then have the children feel their own throats vibrate as they speak. A tuning fork can also be a teaching aid when talking about vibrations.

6. **Telephone Parts**

   Dismantle an old telephone and put it on the science table for the children to discover and explore the parts.

Dramatic Play:

1. **Post Office**

   In the dramatic play area place a mailbox, envelopes, old cards, paper, pens, old stampers, ink pads, hats, and mailbags. During self-selected or self-initiated play periods, the children can play post office.

2. Telephone Booth

Make a telephone booth from a large refrigerator-sized cardboard box. Inside, place a toy phone. Place in the dramatic play area.

3. Television

Obtain a discarded television console to use for puppetry or storytelling experiences. Remove the back and set, leaving just the wooden frame. If desired, make curtains.

4. Radio Station

Place an old microphone, or one made from a styrofoam ball and cardboard, with records in the dramatic play area.

5. Puppet Show

Place a puppet stand and a variety of puppets in the dramatic play area for the children to use during the self-selected or self-directed play period.

Arts and Crafts:

1. Record Player Art

Place a piece of round paper or a paper plate with a hole punched in the center on a record player turntable. Turn the record player on. The children can use crayons or markers to draw softly on the paper while the record player is spinning.

2. Easel Idea

Cut easel paper in the shape of a book, record, radio, or other piece of communication equipment.

3. Traffic Lights

Provide red, yellow, and green circles, glue, and construction paper for the children to create a traffic light.

4. Stationery

Provide the children with various stencils or stamps to make their own stationery. It can be used for a gift for a parent or a special person. Children could then dictate a letter to a relative or friend.

Large Muscle:

Charades

Invite children one at a time to come to the front of the group. Then whisper something in the child's ear, like "You're very happy." The child then uses his hands, face, feet, arms, etc., to communicate this feeling to the other children. The group of children then identifies the demonstrated feeling.

Field Trips/Resource People:

1. Post Office

Visit a local post office. Encourage the children to observe how the mail is sorted.

2. Phone Company

Visit a local phone company.

3. Radio Station

Visit a local disc jockey at the radio station.

4. Television Station

If available, visit a local television station. Observe the cameras, microphones, and other communication devices.

5. Sign Language Demonstration

Invite someone to demonstrate sign language.

Math:

Phone Numbers

Make a list of the children's names and telephone numbers. Place the list by a toy, trainer, or unhooked telephone.

Social Studies:

Thank You

Let the children dictate a group thank-you letter to one of your resource visitors or field trip representatives. Before mailing the letter, provide writing tools for children to sign their names.

Group time (games, language):

1. **Telephone**

   Play the game "telephone" by having the children sit in a circle. Begin by whispering a short phrase into a child's ear. That child whispers your message to the next child. Continue until the message gets to the last child. The last child repeats the message out loud. It is fun to see how much it has changed. (This game is most successful with older children.)

2. **What's Missing?**

   Place items that are related to communication on a tray. Include a stamp, a telephone, a record, a pocket radio, etc. The children can examine the objects for a few minutes. After this they should close their eyes while you remove an object. Then let the children look at the tray and identify which object is missing.

3. **Household Objects Sound Like…**

   Make a tape of different sounds around the house. Include a radio, television, alarm clock, telephone, vacuum cleaner, flushing toilet, door bells, egg timer, etc. Play the tape for the children, letting them identify the individual sounds.

Cooking:

Edible Envelope

Spread peanut butter on a graham cracker. Add raisins to represent an address and a stamp.

FINGERPAINT RECIPES

Liquid Starch Method

liquid starch (put in
   squeeze bottles)
dry tempera paint in
   shakers

Put about 1 tablespoon of
   liquid starch on the
   surface to be painted.
   Let the child shake the
   paint onto the starch.
   Mix and blend the paint.
   Note: If this paint
   becomes too thick,
   simply sprinkle a few
drops of water onto the
painting.

Soap Flake Method

Mix in a small bowl:
soap flakes
a small amount of water

Beat until stiff with an egg-
   beater. Use white soap
   on dark paper, or add
   colored tempera paint to
   the soap and use it on
   light-colored paper. This
   gives a slight three-
   dimensional effect.

Wheat Flour Paste

3 parts water
1 part wheat paste flour
coloring

Stir flour into water. Add
   coloring. (Wallpaper
   paste can be bought at
   low cost in wallpaper
   stores or department
   stores.)

Uncooked Laundry Starch

A mixture of 1 cup laun-
   dry/liquid starch, 1 cup

72

cold water, and 3 cups soap flakes will provide a quick fingerpaint.

Flour and Salt I

1 cup flour
1 1/2 cups salt
3/4 cup water
coloring

Combine flour and salt. Add water. This has a grainy quality, unlike the other fingerpaints, providing a different sensory experience. Some children enjoy the different touch sensation when 1 1/2 cups salt are added to the other recipes.

Flour and Salt II

2 cups flour
2 teaspoons salt
3 cups cold water
2 cups hot water
coloring

Add salt to flour, then pour in cold water gradually and beat mixture with egg beater until it is smooth. Add hot water and boil until it becomes clear. Beat until smooth, then mix in coloring. Use 1/4 cup food coloring to 8 to 9 ounces of paint for strong colors.

Instantized Flour Uncooked Method

1 pint water (2 cups)
1 1/2 cups instantized flour (the kind used to thicken gravy)

Put the water in the bowl and stir the flour into the water. Add color. Regular flour may be lumpy.

Cooked Starch Method

1 cup laundry starch dissolved in a small amount of cold water
5 cups boiling water added slowly to dissolve starch
1 tablespoon glycerine (optional)

Cook the mixture until it is thick and glossy. Add 1 cup mild soap flakes. Add color in separate containers. Cool before using.

Cornstarch Method

Gradually add 2 quarts water to 1 cup cornstarch. Cook until clear and add 1/2 cup soap flakes (like Ivory Snow). A few drops of glycerine or oil of wintergreen may be added.

Flour Method

Mix 1 cup flour and 1 cup cold water. Add 3 cups boiling water and bring all to a boil, stirring constantly. Add 1 tablespoon alum and coloring. Paintings from this recipe dry flat and do not need to be ironed.

TIPS

1. Be sure you have running water and towels nearby or provide a large basin of water where children can rinse off.

2. Fingerpaint on smooth table, oil cloth, or cafeteria tray. Some children prefer to start fingerpainting with shaving cream on a sheet of oil cloth.

3. Food coloring or powdered paint may be added to mixture before using, or allow child to choose the colors he wants sprinkled on top of paint.

4. Sometimes reluctant children are more easily attracted to paint table if the fingerpaints are already colored.

Multimedia:

The following resources can be found in educational catalogs:

1. Jenkins, Ella. *Jambo Songs and Chants* [record].

2. *Community Helpers* [record]. Bowmar/Noble Publishers.

3. Palmer, Hap. *Creative Movement and Rhythmic Exploration* [record].

4. *Listening Skills for Pre-readers* [record]. Classroom Materials, Inc.

5. Jenkins, Ella. *You'll Sing a Song and I'll Sing a Song* [record].

6. *Starting to Read* [54-minute video]. Edu-vid.

7. *Alphie's Alphabet* [60-minute video]. Edu-vid.

8. *Getting Ready to Read* [video]. Random House.

9. *Learning about Letters* [video]. Random House.

10. *Reader Rabbit's Ready for Letters* [IBM/Mac software, PK–1]. The Learning Company.

11. *Reading Maze* [Mac software, PK–2]. Great Wave.

12. *Mario's Early Years: Fun with Letters* [IBM software, PK–1]. Software Tools.

13. *Reading Rodeo* [Apple/IBM/Mac software, PK–1]. Heartsoft.

Books:

The following books can be used to complement the theme:

1. Chaplin, Susan Gibbons. (1986). *I Can Sign My ABC's*. Washington, DC: Gallaudet University Press.

2. Baker, Pamela. (1986). *My First Book of Sign*. Washington, DC: Gallaudet University Press.

3. Kalman, Bobbie. (1986). *How We Communicate*. New York: Crabtree Publishing Company.

4. Hughes, S. (1985). *Noisy*. New York: Lothrop, Lee & Shepard Company.

5. Everett, Louise. (1988). *Amigo Means Friend*. Mahwah, NJ: Troll Associates.

6. Hutchins, Pat. (1991). *The Surprise Party*. New York: Macmillan Children's Book Group.

7. Leedy, Loreen. (1990). *The Furry News: How to Make a Newspaper*. New York: Holiday House, Inc.

8. Brown, Ann. (1992). *TV or Not TV*. Racine, WI: Western Publishing Co.

9. Levine, Ellen. (1989). *I Hate English!* New York: Scholastic.

10. Hayes, Sarah. (1988). *Clap Your Hands: Finger Rhymes*. New York: Lothrop, Lee & Shepard.

11. Bulla, Clyde R. (1989). *Singing Sam*. New York: Random House.

12. Morris, Winifred. (1990). *Just Listen*. New York: Macmillan.

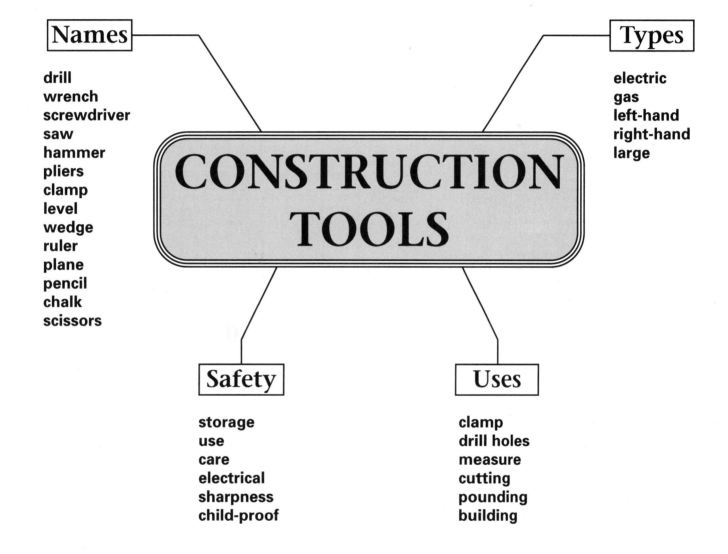

Names

drill
wrench
screwdriver
saw
hammer
pliers
clamp
level
wedge
ruler
plane
pencil
chalk
scissors

Types

electric
gas
left-hand
right-hand
large

CONSTRUCTION TOOLS

Safety

storage
use
care
electrical
sharpness
child-proof

Uses

clamp
drill holes
measure
cutting
pounding
building

Theme Goals:

Through participating in the experiences provided by this theme, the children may learn:

1. Types of tools.

2. Names of common tools.

3. Functions of tools.

4. Tool safety.

Concepts for the Children to Learn:

1. Tools can be electric or hand-powered.

2. Tools are helpful when building.

3. Pliers, tweezers, and clamps hold things.

4. Drills, nails, and screws make holes.

5. Planes, saws, and scissors cut materials.

6. Hammers and screwdrivers are used to put in and remove nails and screws.

7. Rulers are used for measuring.

8. To be safe, tools need to be handled with care.

9. Goggles should be worn to protect our eyes when using tools.

10. After use, tools need to be put away.

Vocabulary:

1. **tool**—an object to help us.

2. **drill**—a tool that cuts holes.

3. **wrench**—a tool that holds things.

4. **screwdriver**—a tool that turns screws.

5. **saw**—a cutting tool with sharp edges.

6. **hammer**—a tool used to insert or remove objects such as nails.

7. **pliers**—a tool used for holding.

8. **clamp**—a tool used to join or hold things.

9. **ruler**—a measuring tool.

10. **wedge**—a tool used for splitting.

11. **plane**—a tool used for shaving wood.

Bulletin Board

The purpose of this bulletin board is to develop awareness of types of tools, as well as foster visual discrimination skills. A shadow tool match bulletin board can be constructed by drawing about six or seven tool pieces on tagboard. See the illustration. These pieces can be colored and cut out. Next, trace the pieces on black construction paper to make shadows of each piece. These shadow pieces can be attached to the bulletin board. Magnet pieces can be applied to both the shadows and the colored tool pieces, or a push pin can be placed above the shadow and a hole can be punched in the colored tool piece. The children can match the colored tool piece to its corresponding-shaped shadow.

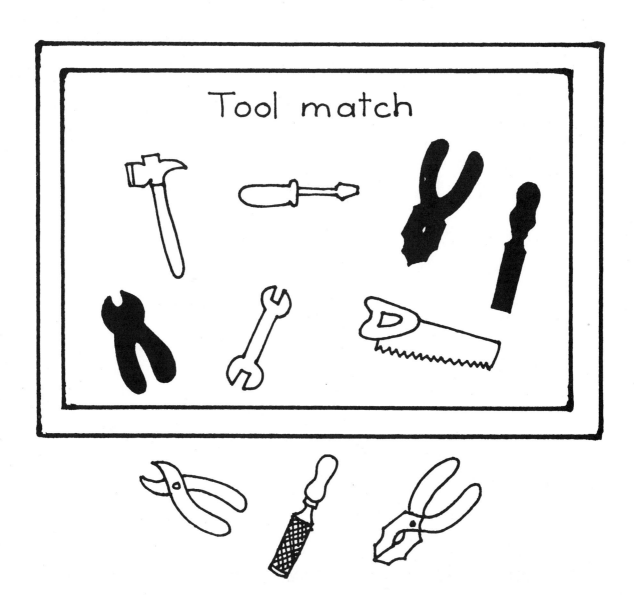

Parent Letter

Dear Parents,

Construction tools will be the focus of our next unit. This unit will help your child become more aware of many kinds of tools, their purposes, and tool safety. While exploring this unit, the children will have opportunities to use many hand tools at the woodworking bench.

At School

Some of the activities the children will participate in include:

- painting with screwdrivers and wrenches.
- exploring wood shavings in the sensory table.
- setting up a mechanic's shop where the children can pretend to fix cars.
- a visit on Wednesday from Mr. Smith, a local shoe repairer. Mr. Smith will show us the tools he uses to repair shoes.

At Home

To develop memory skills, recall with your child all of the tools we use in our homes—from cooking and cleaning tools to gardening tools. Count the number of tools that are in each room of your house. Which room contains the most tools? This will promote the mathematical concepts of rational counting and vocabulary of most and least.

Have fun with your child!

Construction tools help people build tall buildings.

Music:

"This Is the Way"
(Sing to the tune of "Mulberry Bush")

This is the way we saw our wood,
saw our wood, saw our wood.
This is the way we saw our wood,
so early in the morning.

Other verses: pound our nails
drill a hole
use a screwdriver

Fingerplays:

CARPENTER'S HAMMER

The carpenter's hammer goes rap, rap, tap
  (make hammer motion)
And his saw goes see, saw, see.
  (make saw motions)
He planes and measures and hammers and saws
  (act out each one)
While he builds a house for me.
  (draw house with index fingers)

JOHNNY'S HAMMER

Johnny works with one hammer, one hammer, one hammer.
Johnny works with one hammer, then he works with two.

Say the same words adding one hammer each time. Children are to pretend to hammer using various body parts.

Verse 1: 1 hand hitting leg.
Verse 2: 2 hands hitting legs.
Verse 3: use motions for verses 1 and 2, plus tap one foot.
Verse 4: verses 1, 2, and 3 plus tap other foot.
Verse 5: verses 1 to 4, plus nod head. At the end of verse 5 say, "Then he goes to sleep," and place both hands by side of head.

You can also change the name used in the fingerplay to include names of children in your classroom.

THE COBBLER

Cobbler, cobbler, mend my shoe.
  (point to shoe)
Get it done by half past two.
  (hold up two fingers)

Half past two is much too late.
Get it done by half past eight.
   (hold up eight fingers)

Science:

1. **Exploring Levels**

   Place levels and wood scraps on a table for the children to explore while being closely supervised.

2. **Hammers**

   Collect a variety of hammers, various-sized nails, and wood scraps or styrofoam. Allow the children to practice pounding using the different tools and materials.

3. **The Wide World of Rulers**

   Set up a display with different types and sizes of rulers. Include the reel type. Paper and pencils can also be added to create interest.

Dramatic Play:

1. **The Carpenter**

   Place a carpentry box with scissors, rulers, and masking tape in the woodworking area. Also, provide large cardboard boxes and paint, if desired.

2. **Shoemaker Store**

   Set up a shoemaker's store. Provide the children with shoes, toy hammers, smocks, cash registers, and play money. The children can act out mending, buying, and selling shoes.

Arts and Crafts:

1. **Rulers**

   Set rulers and paper on the table. The children can then experiment creating lines and geometric shapes.

2. **Tool Print**

   Pour a small amount of thick colored tempera paint in a flat pan. Also, provide the children with miniature tools such as wrenches, screwdrivers, and paper. The children then can place the tools in the paint pan, remove them, and print on paper.

Sensory:

1. **Scented Playdough**

   Prepare playdough and add a few drops of extract such as peppermint, anise, or almond. Also, collect a variety of scissors, and place in the art area with the playdough.

2. **Wood Shavings**

   Place wood shavings in the sensory table along with scoops and pails.

Large Muscle:

The Workbench

In the woodworking area place various tools, wood, and goggles for the children to use. It is very important to discuss the safety and limits used when at the workbench prior to this activity. An extra adult is helpful to supervise this area.

Field Trips/Resource People:

1. **Shoe Repair Store**

   Visit a shoe repair store. Observe a shoe being repaired.

2. **Wood Worker**

   Invite a parent or other person into the classroom who enjoys woodworking as a hobby.

Math:

1. **Use of Rulers**

   Discuss how rulers are used. Provide children with rulers so that they may measure various objects in the classroom. Allow them to compare the lengths. Also, measure each child and construct a chart including each child's height.

2. **Weighing Tools**

   Place scales and a variety of tools on the math table. Let the children explore weighing the tools.

Social Studies:

1. **Tool Safety**

   Discuss the safe use of tools. Allow the children to help decide what classroom rules are necessary for using tools. Make a chart containing these rules to display in the woodworking area.

2. **Helper Chart**

   Design a helper chart for the children to assist with cleanup and care of the classroom tools. Each day select new children to assist, assuring that everyone gets a turn. To participate, the children can be responsible for cleaning the dirty tools and putting them away.

Group Time (games, language):

1. **Tool of the Day**

   Each day of this unit, introduce a "tool of the day." Explain how each tool is used and who uses it. If possible, leave the tool out for children to use on the woodworking bench.

2. **Thank-You Letter**

   Using a pencil as a tool, let the children dictate a thank-you note to any resource person or field trip site coordinator who has contributed to the program.

Cooking:

"Hands On" Cookies

   3 cups brown sugar
   3 cups margarine or butter
   6 cups oatmeal
   1 tablespoon baking soda
   3 cups flour

   Place all of the ingredients in a bowl. Let the children use clean child-size wooden hammers to mash and knead. Form into small balls and place on ungreased cookie sheet. Butter the bottom of a glass. Dip the bottom of the glass into a saucer with sugar. Use the glass to flatten the balls. Bake in an oven preheated to 350 degrees for 10 to 12 minutes. Makes 15 dozen.

SCIENCE MATERIALS AND EQUIPMENT

Teachers need to continuously provide science materials for the classroom. Materials that can be collected include:

acorns and other nuts	bones	drinking straws
aluminum foil	bowls and cups	drums
ball bearings	cocoon	egg cartons
balloons	corks	eggbeaters
binoculars	discorded clock	eyedroppers and basters
bird nests	dishpans	fabric scraps

filter paper	musical instruments	scales
flashlight	newspapers	scissors—assorted sizes
flowers	nails, screws, bolts	screen wire
gears	paper bags	sieves, sifters, and funnels
insect nests	paper of various types	seeds
insects	paper rolls and spools	spatulas
jacks	plants	sponges
kaleidoscope	plastic bags	stones
locks and keys	plastic containers with	string
magnets—varying	lids—many sizes	styrofoam
strengths, sizes	plastic tubing	tape
magnifying glasses—good	pots, pans, trays, muffin	thermometers
lenses	tins	tongs and tweezers
marbles	prisms	tools—hammer, pliers
measuring cups and	pulleys	tuning forks
spoons	rocks	waxed paper
microscope	rubber tubing	weeds
milk cartons	ruler	wheels
mirrors—all sizes	safety goggles—child size	wood and other building
moths	sandpaper	materials

Multimedia:

The following resources can be found in educational catalogs:

1. *Moving Machines* [25-minute video]. Bo Peep Productions.

2. *Alphabet Blocks* [IBM/Mac/Windows software, PK–1]. Bright Star.

Books:

The following books can be used to complement the theme:

1. Screckhise, Roseva. (1985). *What Was It Before It Was a Chair?* Chicago: Children's Press.

2. Jennings, Terry. (1993). *Cranes, Dump Trucks, Bulldozers and Other Building Machines.* New York: Kingfisher Books

3. Krasilovsky, Phyllis. (1992). *The Man Who Was Too Lazy to Fix Things.* New York: William Morrow and Co.

4. Miller, Margaret. (1990). *Who Uses This?* New York: Greenwillow Books.

5. Sandow, Lyn. (1990). *My Drill.* New York: Little, Brown and Co.

6. Sandow, Lyn. (1990). *My Pliers.* New York: Little, Brown and Co.

7. Sandow, Lyn. (1990). *My Saw*. New York: Little, Brown and Co.

8. Sandow, Lyn. (1990). *My Screwdriver*. New York: Little, Brown and Co.

9. Sandow, Lyn. (1990). *My Wrench*. New York: Little, Brown and Co.

10. Stone, Venice. (1991). *Tools*. New York: Scholastic, Inc.

11. *Ernie's Little Toolbook: A Sesame Street Book*. (1991). New York: Random House Books for Young Readers.

12. Morris, Ann. (1992). *Tools*. New York: Lothrop, Lee & Shepard.

13. Butterworth, Brent, & Green, Tie. (1991). *The Big Book of How Things Work*. Lincolnwood, IL: Publications International.

14. Macauley, David. (1988). *The Way Things Work*. Boston: Houghton Mifflin.

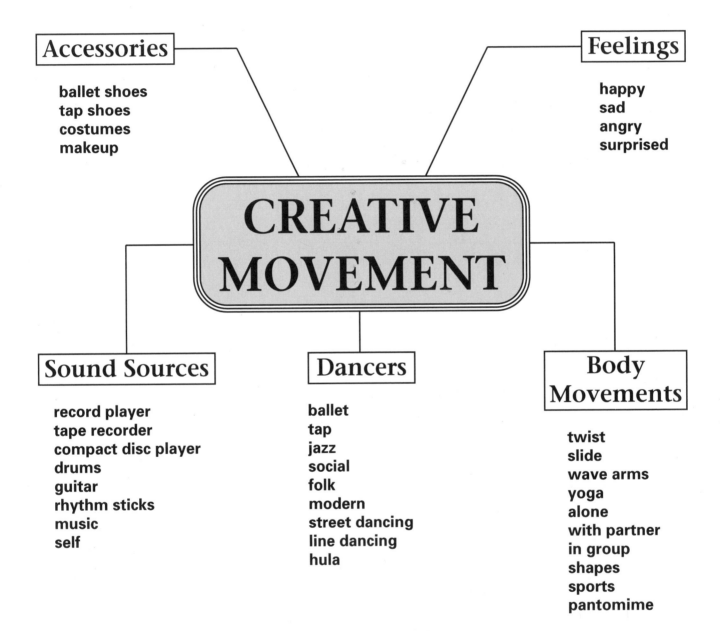

Accessories

- ballet shoes
- tap shoes
- costumes
- makeup

Feelings

- happy
- sad
- angry
- surprised

CREATIVE MOVEMENT

Sound Sources

- record player
- tape recorder
- compact disc player
- drums
- guitar
- rhythm sticks
- music
- self

Dancers

- ballet
- tap
- jazz
- social
- folk
- modern
- street dancing
- line dancing
- hula

Body Movements

- twist
- slide
- wave arms
- yoga
- alone
- with partner
- in group
- shapes
- sports
- pantomime

Theme Goals:

Through participating in the experiences provided by this theme, the children may learn:

1. Creative movement accessories.

2. Creative movement sound sources.

3. Body movements used in creative movement.

4. Expression of feelings through creative movement.

5. Types of dancers.

Concepts for the Children to Learn:

1. People can dance to music.

2. The record player, tape recorder, and compact disc player are all sound sources used for dance.

3. Dancing and moving can be done alone, with a partner, or in a group.

4. Our bodies can move in many different ways.

5. Ballet, tap, jazz, and social are some types of dances.

6. Happy, sad, angry, and surprised are feelings that can be expressed through dance.

7. Some dancers wear special costumes and makeup.

8. Ballet and tap dancers wear special shoes.

9. Our bodies can move to the sound of drums, guitars, and rhythm sticks.

10. We can twist, slide, and wave our arms during dance.

Vocabulary:

1. **dance**—a pattern of body movements.

2. **movement**—change in body position.

3. **ballet**—movement that usually tells a story.

4. **music**—sounds made by instruments or voices.

Bulletin Board

The purpose of this bulletin board is to develop one-to-one correspondence skills and the ability to match a set to the matching written numeral. Construct tank tops, each a different color, from a sheet of tagboard. See the illustration. Print a numeral that would be developmentally appropriate for the group of children on each tank top. Draw a corresponding number of black dots below each numeral. Construct a tutu ruffle from white tagboard for each top. Place colored dots on each ruffle. Trace ruffles onto black construction paper. Laminate all pieces. Staple tank tops and shadow ruffles to bulletin board. The children can match the ruffles with dots to the corresponding tank top, using holes in white ruffles and push pins in shadow ruffles.

Parent Letter

Dear Parents,

Children love to dance, and they are constantly on the move. We will begin a unit on creative movement. Throughout the activities provided in the unit the children will discover the different ways our bodies move, and also learn about various forms of dance. Some of the activities include:

- singing songs and moving to music.
- dancing in the dance studio that will be set up in the dramatic play area.
- watching other people move.
- participating in an aerobics class.

Field Trip

On Thursday, at 2:30 p.m., we will be taking a bus to a dance studio. At the studio, we will observe dancers and learn a few steps from a dance instructor. To assist with the trip, we need several parents to accompany us. Please call the school if you are available.

At Home

As your child develops, he will show increased control and interest in perfecting and improving motor skills. To foster the development of large muscle skills, balance, and body coordination, provide opportunities each day for vigorous play. Give suggestions, such as "How fast can you hop?" "How far can you hop on one foot?" etc. Also, ask your child to walk on a curved line, a straight line, or a balance beam.

Enjoy your child!

Exercise can be a form of creative movement.

Fingerplays:

The following circle games are from *Finger Frolics: Fingerplays for Young Children* by Cromwell, Hibner, and Faitel. (Partner Press: 1983).

HOP AND TWIRL

Make a circle and we'll go around.
First walk on tiptoe so we don't make a sound.
Tip, toe, around we go.
Then hop on our left foot, and then on our right.
Then hop together. What a funny sight!
Now stop hopping and twirl around
Now we're ready to settle down.

A CIRCLE

Around in a circle we will go.
Little tiny baby steps, make us go very slow.

And then we'll take some great giant steps,
As big as they can be.
Then in our circle we'll stand quietly.

STAND IN A CIRCLE

Stand in a circle and clap your hands.
Clap, clap, clap, clap.
Now put your hands over your head.
Slap, slap, slap, slap.
Now hands at your sides and turn around.
Then in our circle we'll all sit down.

ONE TO TEN CIRCLE

Let's make a circle and around we go,
Not too fast and not too slow.
One, two, three, four, five, six, seven, eight,
nine, ten,
Let's face the other way and go around again.
One, two, three, four, five, six, seven, eight,
nine, ten.

PARTNER GAME

Pick a partner, take a hand.
Then in a circle partners stand.
Take two steps forward,
And two steps back.
Then bow to your partner
And clap, clap, clap.
Wrap your elbows
And around you go.
Not too fast and not too slow.
Change elbows.
Go around again.
Then stand in a circle
And count to ten.

Science:

1. **Magnet Dancers**

    On a piece of tagboard, draw pictures of three-inch dancers. Stickers or pictures from magazines can also be used. Cut the dancers out and attach paper clips to the back side. Use a small box and a magnet to make these dancers move. Hold the dancers up on one side of the box and move the dancer up by holding and moving a magnet on the other side of the box.

2. **Kaleidoscopes**

On the science table, put a number of kaleidoscopes. The tiny figures inside appear to be dancing.

3. **Dancing Shoes**

Place various types of dancing shoes at the science table. Let the children compare the shape, size, color, and texture of the shoes. The children may also enjoy trying the shoes on for size and dancing in them.

Dramatic Play:

1. **Dance Studio**

Add to the dramatic play area tap shoes, tutus, ballet shoes, tights, and leotards. Provide a record player with records or tape player with tapes.

2. **Fitness Gym**

Add to the dramatic play area a small mat, head bands, wrist bands, sweat shirts, sweat pants, leotards, and music.

Arts and Crafts:

1. **Stencils**

The teacher can construct stencils from tagboard. Shapes such as shoes, ballerinas, circles, etc., can be made and added to the art table for use during self-selected activity periods.

2. **Musical Painting**

Provide a tape recorder with headphones and a tape of children's music or classical music at the easel. The children can listen and move their brushes to the music, if desired.

Large Muscle:

1. **Streamer/Music Activity**

In the music area provide streamers. Play a variety of music, allowing the children, if desired, to move to the different rhythms.

2. **Do As I Say**

Provide the children verbal cues for moving. For example, say, "Move like you are sad," "Show me that you are tired," "You just received a special present," or "Show me how you feel."

3. **Animal Movement**

Ask a child to act out the way a certain animal moves. Examples include: frog, spider, caterpillar, butterfly, etc.

4. **Balance**

Add a balance beam or balance strip to the indoor or outdoor environment.

5. **Roly-Poly**

The children can stretch their bodies out on the floor. When touched by a teacher, the child rolls into a tight ball.

6. **Dancing Cloud**

Using an inflated white balloon or ball, let the children stand in a circle and bounce or hit it to each other.

7. **Obstacle Course**

Set up an obstacle course indoors or outdoors depending on the weather. Let the children move their bodies in many different ways. They can run or crawl through the course. Older children may enjoy hopping or skipping.

Field Trips/Resource People:

1. **Field Trips**

- dance studio
- health club
- gymnasium

2. **Resource People**

Invite the following people to class to talk with the children:

- a dancer or dance instructor
- gymnast
- aerobics instructor

Math:

1. Matching Leotards to Hangers

Using plastic hangers, prepare a numeral on each of the hangers. Provide the children with a box of leotards. Have a printed numeral on each. Encourage the children to match the numbered leotard with the identically numbered hanger.

2. Following Steps

Using tagboard, cut out some left feet and right feet. Write the numerals from one to ten on the feet and arrange them in numerical order. Place the footprints on the floor, securing them with masking tape. Encourage the children to begin the walk on the numeral one and continue in the correct sequence.

3. Ballet Puzzle

Purchase a large poster of a ballet dancer. Laminate the poster or cover it with clear contact paper. Cut the poster into several large shapes. Place the puzzle in the manipulative area. During self-selected play periods, the children can reconstruct the puzzle.

Social Studies:

Social Dancing

Let each child choose a partner. Encourage the children to hold hands. Play music as a background, so the partners can move together.

Group Time (games, language):

1. Balloon Bounce

Blow up balloons for the children to use at group time. Play music and have children bounce the balloons up in the air. Let the balloons float to the ground when the music ends. Supervision is required for this activity. Broken balloons should be immediately removed from the environment.

2. Toy Movements

Form a circle and move like different toys. Try to include as many actual toys as you can, so that the children can observe each toy moving, and then can more easily pretend to be that toy.

- jack-in-the-box
- wind-up dolls
- roll like a ball
- skates

3. Rag Doll

Repeat the following poem as the child creates a dance with a rag doll.

If I were a rag doll
And I belonged to you,
Whenever I would try to dance,
This is what I'd do.

Cooking:

1. Orange Buttermilk Smoothie

1 quart buttermilk
3 cups orange juice
1/2 teaspoon cinnamon
1/4 cup honey

Blend in a blender until the mixture is smooth. Enjoy!

2. Indian Flat Bread

2 cups all-purpose flour
1/4 cup unflavored yogurt
1 egg, slightly beaten
1 1/2 teaspoons baking powder
1 teaspoon sugar
1/4 teaspoon salt
1/4 teaspoon baking soda
1/2 cup milk
vegetable oil
poppy seeds

Mix all ingredients except milk, vegetable oil, and poppy seeds. Stir in enough milk to make a soft dough. Turn dough onto lightly floured surface. Knead until smooth, about 5 minutes.

90

Place in greased bowl; turn greased side up. Cover and let rest in warm place 3 hours.

Divide dough into 6 or 8 equal parts. Flatten each part on lightly floured surface, rolling it into 6-inch x 4-inch leaf shape about 1/4 inch thick. Brush with vegetable oil; sprinkle with poppy seeds.

Place 2 cookie sheets in oven; heat oven to 450 degrees. Remove hot cookie sheets from oven; place breads on cookie sheets. Bake until firm, 6 to 8 minutes. Makes 6 to 8 breads.

Source: *Betty Crocker's International Cookbook.* (1980). New York: Random House.

MOVEMENT ACTIVITIES

Listen to the Drum

Accessory: drum
fast
slow
heavy
soft
big
small

Choose a Partner

Make a big shape
go over
go under
go through
go around

To Become Aware of Time

Run very fast
Walk very slowly
Jump all over the floor quickly
Sit down on the floor slowly
Slowly grow up as tall as you can
Slowly curl up on the floor as small as possible

To Become Aware of Space

Lift your leg up in front of you
Lift it up backwards, sideways
Lift your leg and step forward, backwards, sideways, and around and around

Reach up to the ceiling
Stretch to touch the walls
Punch down to the floor

To Become Aware of Weight

To feel the difference between heavy and light, the child should experiment with his own body force.
Punch down to the floor hard
Lift your arms up slowly and gently
Stomp on the floor
Walk on tiptoe
Kick out one leg as hard as you can
Very smoothly and lightly slide one foot along the floor

Moving Shapes

1. Try to move about like something huge and heavy: elephant, tug boat, bulldozer.
2. Try to move like something small and heavy: a fat frog, a heavy top.
3. Try moving like something big and light: a beach ball, a parachute, a cloud.
4. Try moving like something small and light: a feather, a snowflake, a flea, a butterfly.

Put Yourself Inside Something

(bottle, box, barrel)
You're *outside* of something—now get into it
You're *inside* of something—now get out of it
You're *underneath* something
You're *on top of* something
You're *beside* or *next to* something
You're *surrounded* by it

Pantomime

1. You're going to get a present. What is the shape of the box? How big is the box? Feel it. Hold it. Unwrap it. Take it out. Put it back in.
2. Think about an occupation. How does the worker act?
3. Show me that it is cold, hot.
4. You are two years old (sixteen, eighty, etc.)
5. Show me: It's very early in the morning, late in the afternoon.
6. Show me: What is the weather like?
7. Pretend you are driving, typing, raking leaves.
8. Take a partner. Pretend you're playing ball.

Multimedia:

The following resources can be found in educational catalogs:

1. Nelson, Esther, & Haack, Bruce. *Dance, Sing, and Listen* [record].

2. Palmer, Hap. *Creative Movement and Rhythmic Exploration* [record].

3. Jenkins, Ella. *Songs, Rhythms and Chants for the Dance* [record].

4. *Music for Creative Movement* [record]. Kimbo Records.

5. *Simple Folk Dances* [record]. Kimbo Records.

6. *Tempo for Tots* [record]. Melody House.

7. *Preschool Fitness* [record]. Melody House.

8. *Channel 3* [record]. Melody House.

9. *Up & Down, In & Out, Big & Little* [30-minute video]. Edu-vid.

10. *Mario's Early Years: Preschool Fun* [IBM software, PK–1]. Software Tools.

Books:

The following books can be used to complement the theme:

1. Raffi. (1987). *Shake My Sillies Out*. New York: Crown Publishers, Inc.

2. Jonas, Ann. (1989). *Color Dance*. New York: Greenwillow Books.

3. Alpert, Lou. (1991). *Emma's Turn to Dance*. Ipswich, MA: Whispering Coyote Press.

4. Jabar, Cynthia (Comp.). (1992). *Shimmy Shake Earthquake: Don't Forget to Dance Poems*. New York: Little, Brown and Co.

5. Nicklaus, Carol. (1991). *Come Dance with Me*. Eden Prairie, MN: Silver Press.

6. Slater, Teddy. (1992). *The Bunny Hop*. New York: Scholastic, Inc.

7. Martin, Bill, Jr., & Archambalt, John. (1986). *Barn Dance*. New York: Henry Holt & Company.

8. Coombs, Linda. (1992). *Pow Wow*. Cleveland, OH: Modern Curriculum Press.

9. Brown, Marc. (1985). *Hand Rhymes*. New York: E. P. Dutton.

10. Oxenbury, Helen. (1987). *All Fall Down*. New York: Macmillan.

11. Ackerman, Karen. (1988). *Song and Dance Man*. New York: Alfred A. Knopf.

12. Shannon, George. (1991). *Dance Away*. New York: Morrow.

13. Giff, Patricia R. (1989). *The Almost Awful Play*. New York: Live Oak Media.

14. Brown, Judith G. (1989). *The Mask of the Dancing Princess*. New York: Macmillan.

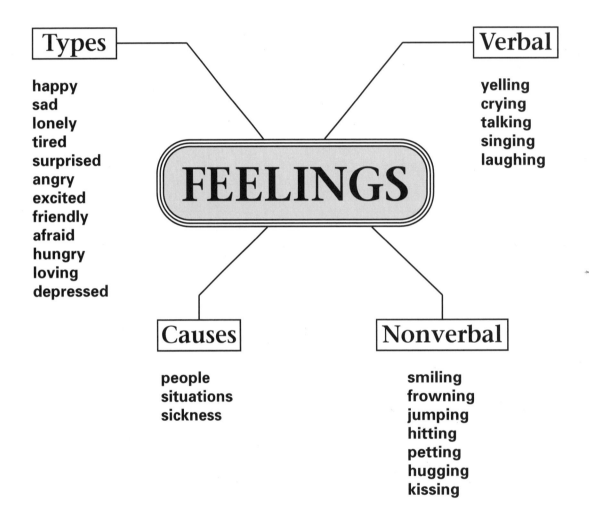

Types
happy
sad
lonely
tired
surprised
angry
excited
friendly
afraid
hungry
loving
depressed

Verbal
yelling
crying
talking
singing
laughing

FEELINGS

Causes
people
situations
sickness

Nonverbal
smiling
frowning
jumping
hitting
petting
hugging
kissing

Theme Goals:

Through participating in the experiences provided by this theme, the children may learn:

1. Types of feelings.

2. Verbal expressions of feelings.

3. Nonverbal expressions of feelings.

4. Causes for our feelings.

Concepts for the Children to Learn:

1. Everyone has feelings.

2. Feelings show how we feel.

3. Feelings change.

4. Happy, sad, excited, and surprised are types of feelings.

5. Happy people usually smile.

6. Sad people sometimes cry.

Vocabulary:

1. **feelings**—expressed emotions.

2. **happy**—a feeling of being glad.

3. **smile**—a facial expression of pleasure or happiness.

4. **surprise**—a feeling from something unexpected.

5. **sad**—the feeling of being hurt or unhappy.

6. **afraid**—the feeling of being unsure of or frightened about something.

Bulletin Board

The purpose of this bulletin board is to help the children become aware of feelings, as well as recognize their printed names. Prepare individual name cards for each child. Then prepare different expression faces such as happy, sad, and angry. Staple faces to top of bulletin board. See the illustration for an example. If available, magnetic strips may be added to the bulletin board under faces and pieces affixed to name cards, or push pins may be placed on the board and holes punched in name cards. The children may place their names under the face they decide they feel when arriving at school. Later, during large group time, the board can be reviewed to see if any of the children's feelings have changed.

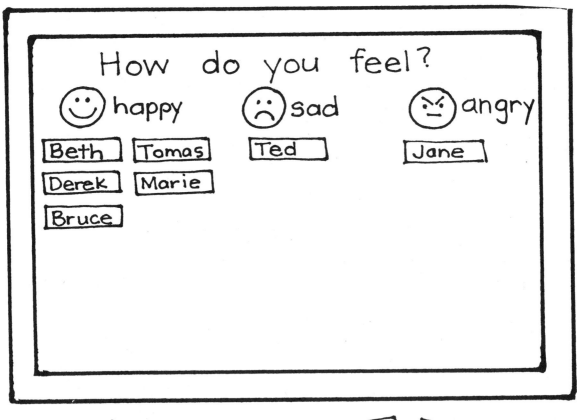

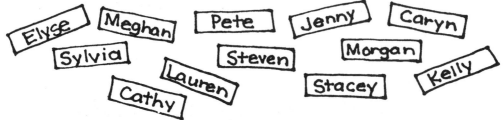

Parent Letter

Dear Parents,

Emotions and feelings will be the focus of our next unit. Throughout each day, the children experience many feelings, ranging from happiness to sadness. The purpose of this unit is to have the children develop an understanding of feelings. Feelings are something we all share, and feelings are acceptable. We will also be exploring ways of expressing different feelings.

At School

Some of the learning experiences planned for this unit include:

- listening and discussing the book, *Alexander and the Terrible, Horrible, No Good, Very Bad Day* by Judith Viorst.
- singing songs about our feelings.
- drawing and painting to various types of music.

Our Special Visitor

"Clancy the Clown" will be visiting the children on Thursday at 3:00 p.m. The children are all looking forward to this special visitor. You are encouraged to join us and share their excitement.

At Home

To help your child identify situations that elicit feelings, have your child cut or tear pictures from discarded magazines that depict events or situations that make your child feel happy or sad. These pictures can then be glued or pasted on paper to create a feelings collage.

Talking with your child about your feelings will encourage parent-child communication. Tell your child what things make you feel various ways. Then ask your child to share some feelings.

Make your child happy today!

How do you feel today?

Music:

1. **"Feelings"**
    (Sing to the tune of "Twinkle, Twinkle Little Star")

    I have feelings.
    You do, too.
    Let's all sing about a few.

    I am happy.
      (smile)
    I am sad.
      (frown)
    I get scared.
      (wrap arms around self)
    I get mad.
      (make a fist and shake it)

    I am proud of being me.
      (hands on hips)
    That's a feeling too you see.

I have feelings.
  (point to self)
You do, too.
  (point to someone else)
We just sang about a few.

2. **"If You're Happy and You Know It"**
    (traditional)

    If you're happy and you know it
    Clap your hands.
      (clap twice)
    If you're happy and you know it
    Clap your hands.
      (clap twice)
    If you're happy and you know it
    Then your face will surely show it.
    If you're happy and you know it
    Clap your hands.
      (clap twice)

    For additional verses, change the emotions and actions.

Fingerplays:

FEELINGS

Smile when you're happy.
Cry when you are sad.
Giggle if it's funny.
Get angry if you're mad.

Source: Wilems, Dick. *Everyday Circle Times.*

I LOOKED INSIDE MY LOOKING GLASS

I looked inside my looking glass
To see what I could see.
It looks like I'm happy today,
Because that smiling face is me.

STAND UP TALL

Stand up tall
Hands in the air.
Now sit down
In your chair.
Clap your hands
And make a frown.
Smile and smile.
Hop like a clown.

Science:

1. **Sound Tape**

   Tape various noises that express emotions; suggestions include sounds such as laughter, cheering, growling, shrieking, crying, etc. Play these sounds for the children letting them identify the emotion. They may also want to act out the emotion.

2. **Communication Without Words**

   Hang a large screen or sheet with a bright light behind it. The children can go behind the screen and act out various emotions. Other children guess how they are feeling.

3. **How Does It Feel?**

   Add various pieces of textured materials to the science table. Include materials such as soft fur, sandpaper, rocks, and cotton. Encourage the children to touch each object and explain how it feels.

Dramatic Play:

1. **Flower Shop**

   Plastic flowers, vases, and wrapping paper can be placed in the dramatic play area. Make a sign that says "Flower Shop." The children may want to arrange, sell, deliver, and receive flowers among one another.

2. **Post Office**

   Collect discarded greeting cards and envelopes. The children can stamp and deliver the cards to one another.

3. **Puppet Center**

   A puppet center can be added to the dramatic play area. Include a variety of puppets and a stage.

Arts and Crafts:

1. **Drawing to Music**

   Play various types of music including jazz, classical, and rock and let the children draw during the self-selected activity period. Different tunes and melodies might make us feel a certain way.

2. **Playdough**

   Using playdough is a wonderful way to vent feelings. Prepare several types and let the children feel the different textures. Color each type a different color. Add a scent to one and to another add a textured material such as sawdust, rice, or sand. A list of playdoughs can be found later in this theme.

3. **Footprints**

   Mix tempera paint. Pour the paint into a shallow jelly roll pan approximately 1/4 inch deep. The children can dip their feet into the pan. After this, they can step directly onto paper. Using their feet as an application tool, footsteps can be made. This activity actually could be used to create a mural to hang in the hall or lobby.

Sensory:

Texture Feelings

Various textures can create feelings. Let the children express their feelings by adding the following to the sensory table:

- cotton
- water (warm or with ice)
- black water
- blue water
- sand
- pebbles
- dirt with scoops
- plastic worms with water

Large Muscle:

1. Mirrors

The children should sit as pairs facing each other. Select one child to make a "feeling face" at the partner. Let the other child guess what feeling it is. A variation of this activity would be to have partners face each other. When one child smiles, the partner is to imitate his feelings.

2. Simon Says

Play "Simon Says" using emotions:
"Simon Says walk in a circle feeling happy…"
"Simon Says walk in a circle feeling sad…"

Resource People:

1. A Clown

Invite a clown to the classroom. You may ask the clown to dress and apply makeup for the children. After the clown leaves, provide makeup for the children.

2. Musician

Invite a musician to play a variety of music for the children to express feelings.

3. Florist

Invite a florist to visit your classroom and show how flowers are arranged. Talk about why people send flowers. If convenient the children could visit the florist, touring the greenhouses.

Math:

Face Match

Collect two small shoe boxes. On one shoe box draw a happy face. On the other box, draw a sad face. Cut faces of people from magazines. The children can sort the pictures accordingly.

Social Studies:

Pictures

Share pictures of individuals engaged in different occupations such as doctors, fire fighters, beauticians, florists, nurses, bakers, etc. Discuss how these individuals help us and how they make us feel.

Group Time (games, language):

Happy Feeling

Discuss happiness. Ask each child one thing that makes him happy. Record each answer on a "Happiness Chart." Post the chart for the parents to observe as they pick up their children.

Cooking:

1. Happy Rolls

1 package of fast-rising dry yeast
1 cup warm water
1/3 cup sugar
1/3 cup cooking oil
3 cups flour
a dash of salt

Measure the warm water and pour it into a bowl. Sprinkle the yeast on top of the water. Let the yeast settle into the water. Mix all of the ingredients in a large bowl. Place the dough on a floured board to knead it. Demonstrate how to knead, letting each of the children take turns kneading the bread. This is a wonderful activity to work through emotions. After kneading it for about 10 minutes, put the ball of dough into a greased bowl. If kneaded sufficiently, the top of the dough should have blisters on it. Cover the bowl and put in the sun or near heat. Let it rise for about an hour or until doubled. Take the dough out of the bowl. Punch it down, knead for several more minutes and then divide the dough into 12 to 15 pieces. Roll each piece of dough into a ball. Place each ball on a greased cookie sheet. Let the dough rise again until doubled. Bake at 450 degrees for 10 to 12 minutes. A happy face can be drawn on the roll with frosting.

2. **Berry "Happy" Shake—Finland**

10 fresh strawberries or 6 tablespoons sliced
   strawberries in syrup, thawed
2 cups cold milk
1 1/2 tablespoons sugar or honey

Wash the strawberries (if fresh) and cut out the stems. Cut the strawberries into small pieces. (If you are using frozen strawberries, drain the syrup into a small bowl or cup and save it.) Pour the milk into the mixing bowl. Add the strawberries. If you are using fresh strawberries, add the sugar or honey. If you are using frozen strawberries, add 3 tablespoons of the strawberry syrup instead of sugar. Beat with the egg beater for 1 minute. Pour the drink into glasses.

Source: Touff, Terry, & Ratner, Marilyn. (1974). *Many Hands Cooking*. New York: Thomas Y. Crowell Company.

3. **Danish Smile Berry Pudding**

1 10-ounce package frozen raspberries, thawed
1 10-ounce package frozen strawberries,
   thawed
1/4 cup cornstarch
2 tablespoons sugar
1/2 cup cold water
1 tablespoon lemon juice
slivered almonds

Puree berries in blender or press through sieve. Mix cornstarch and sugar in 1 1/2-quart saucepan. Gradually stir in water; add puree. Heat to boiling, stirring constantly. Boil and stir 1 minute. Remove from heat. Stir in lemon juice. Pour into dessert dishes or serving bowl. Cover and refrigerate at least 2 hours. Sprinkle with almonds; serve with half-and-half if desired. Makes 6 servings.

Source: *Betty Crocker's International Cookbook*. (1980). New York: Random House.

RECIPES FOR DOUGHS AND CLAYS

Clay Dough

3 cups flour
3 cups salt
3 tablespoons alum

Combine ingredients and slowly add water, a little at a time. Mix well with spoon. As mixture thickens, continue mixing with your hands until it has the feel of clay. If it feels too dry, add more water. If it is too sticky, add equal parts of flour and salt.

Play Dough

2 cups flour
1 cup salt
1 cup hot water
2 tablespoons cooking oil
4 teaspoons cream of tartar
food coloring

Mix well. Knead until smooth. This dough may be kept in a plastic bag or covered container and used again. If it gets sticky, more flour may be added.

Favorite Playdough

Combine and boil until
   dissolved:

2 cups water
1/2 cup salt
food coloring or tempera
   paint

Mix in while very hot:

2 tablespoons cooking oil
2 tablespoons alum
2 cups flour

Knead (approximately 5 minutes) until smooth. Store in covered airtight containers.

Oatmeal Dough

2 cups oatmeal
1 cup flour
1/2 cup water

Combine ingredients. Knead well. This dough has a very different texture, is easily manipulated, and looks different. Finished projects can be painted when dry.

Baker's Clay #1

1 cup cornstarch
2 cups baking soda
1 1/2 cups cold water

Combine ingredients. Stir until smooth. Cook over medium heat, stirring constantly until mixture reaches the consistency of slightly dry mashed potatoes.

Turn out onto plate or bowl, covering with damp cloth. When cool enough to handle, knead thoroughly until smooth and pliable on cornstarch-covered surface.

Store in tightly closed plastic bag or covered container.

Baker's Clay #2

4 cups flour
1 1/2 cups water
1 cup salt

Combine ingredients. Mix well. Knead 5 to 10 minutes. Roll out to 1/4-inch thickness. Cut with decorative cookie cutters or with a knife. Make a hole at the top.

Bake at 250 degrees for 2 hours or until hard. When cool, paint with tempera paint and spray with clear varnish or paint with acrylic paint.

Cloud Dough

3 cups flour
1 cup oil
scent (oil of peppermint, wintergreen, lemon, etc.)
food coloring

Combine ingredients. Add water until easily manipulated (about 1/2 cup).

Sawdust Dough

2 cups sawdust
3 cups flour
1 cup salt

Combine ingredients. Add water as needed. This dough becomes very hard and is not easily broken. It is good to use for making objects and figures that one desires to keep.

Salt Dough

4 cups salt
1 cup cornstarch

Combine with sufficient water to form a paste. Cook over medium heat, stirring constantly.

Peanut Butter Playdough

2 1/2 cups peanut butter
2 tablespoons honey
2 cups powdered milk

Mix well with very clean hands. Keep adding

powdered milk until the dough feels soft, not sticky. This is a dough that can be eaten.

Variations:

1. Cocoa or carob powder can be added for chocolate flavor.
2. Raisins, miniature marshmallows, or chopped peanuts may be added or used to decorate finished shapes.

Each child can be given dough to manipulate and then eat.

Cooked Clay Dough

1 cup flour
1/2 cup cornstarch
4 cups water
1 cup salt
3 or 4 pounds flour
coloring if desired

Stir slowly and be patient with this recipe. Blend the flour and cornstarch with cold water. Add salt to the water and boil. Pour the boiling salt and water solution into the flour and cornstarch paste and cook over hot water until clear. Add the flour and coloring to the cooked solution and knead. After the clay has been in use, if too moist, add flour; if dry, add water. Keep in covered container. Wrap dough with damp cloth or towel. This dough has a very nice texture and is very popular with all age groups. May be kept 2 or 3 weeks.

Play Dough

5 cups flour
2 cups salt
4 tablespoons cooking oil
add water to right consistency

Powdered tempera may be added in with flour, or food coloring may be added to finished dough. This dough may be kept in plastic bag or covered container for approximately 2 to 4 weeks. It is better used as playdough rather than leaving objects to harden.

Used Coffee Grounds

2 cups used coffee grounds
1/2 cup salt
1 1/2 cups oatmeal

Combine ingredients and add enough water to moisten. Children like to roll, pack, and pat this mixture. It has a very different feel and look, but it's not good for finished products. It has a very nice texture.

Mud Dough

2 cups mud
2 cups sand
1/2 cup salt

Combine ingredients and add enough water to make pliable. Children like to work with this mixture. It has a nice texture and is easy to use. This cannot be picked up to save for finished products easily. It can be used for rolling and cutouts.

Soap Modeling

2 cups soap flakes

Add enough water to moisten and whip until consistency to mold. Use soap such as Ivory Snow, Dreft, Lux, etc. Mixture will have very slight flaky appearance when it can be molded. It is very enjoyable for all age groups and is easy to work. Also, the texture is very different from other materials ordinarily used for molding. It may be put up to dry, but articles are very slow to dry.

Soap and Sawdust

1 cup whipped soap
1 cup sawdust

Mix well together. This gives a very different feel and appearance. It is quite easily molded into different shapes by all age groups. May be used for 2 to 3 days if stored in tight plastic bag.

Multimedia:

The following resources can be found in educational catalogs:

1. Rosenshontz, Gary & Bill. *Tickles You* [record].

2. Palmer, Hap. *Happy Hour* [record].

3. *I'm Glad I'm Me* [video]. Random House.

Books:

The following books can be used to complement the theme:

1. Keyworth, C. L. (1986). *New Day*. New York: Morrow.

2. Lionni, Leo. (1986). *It's Mine—A Fable*. New York: Alfred A. Knopf.

3. Amos, Janine. (1991). *Afraid*. Madison, NJ: Raintree Steck—Vaughn Publishing.

4. Amos, Janine. (1991). *Angry*. Madison, NJ: Raintree Steck—Vaughn Publishing.

5. Amos, Janine. (1991). *Hurt*. Madison, NJ: Raintree Steck—Vaughn Publishing.

6. Amos, Janine. (1991). *Jealous*. Madison, NJ: Raintree Steck—Vaughn Publishing.

7. Amos, Janine. (1991). *Lonely*. Madison, NJ: Raintree Steck—Vaughn Publishing.

8. Amos, Janine. (1991). *Sad*. Madison, NJ: Raintree Steck—Vaughn Publishing.

9. Dombrower, Jan. (1990). *Getting to Know Your Feelings*. Pleasanton, CA: Heartwise Press.

10. Moddy, Marlys. (1991). *ABC Books of Feelings*. Saint Louis, MO: Concordia Publishing House.

11. Modesitt, Jeanne. (1992). *Sometimes I Feel Like a Mouse*. New York: Scholastic, Inc.

12. Colin, Susan, & Friedman, Susan Levine. (1991). *Nathan's Day at Preschool*. Seattle, WA: Parenting Press.

13. Carlson, Nancy. (1988). *I Like Me!* New York: Viking Kestrel.

14. Hazen, Barbara Shook. (1992). *Even If I Did Something Awful*. New York: Macmillan.

15. Hines, Anna Grossnickle. (1988). *Grandma Gets Grumpy*. New York: Clarion.

16. Morris, Ann. (1990). *Loving*. New York: Lothrop, Lee, & Shepard.

17. Simon, Norma. (1986). *The Saddest Time*. Niles, IL: Albert Whitman.

18. Wilhelm, Hans. (1985). *I'll Always Love You*. New York: Crown.

19. Prelutsky, Jack (Ed.). (1991). *For Laughing Out Loud: Poems to Tickle Your Funnybone*. New York: Alfred A. Knopf.

20. Duncan, Riana. (1989). *When Emily Woke Up Angry*. New York: Barron.

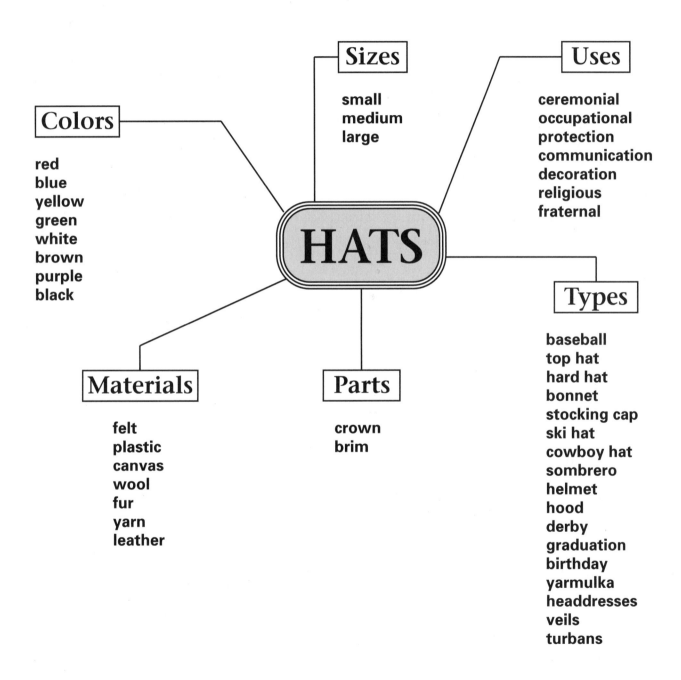

Sizes

small
medium
large

Uses

ceremonial
occupational
protection
communication
decoration
religious
fraternal

Colors

red
blue
yellow
green
white
brown
purple
black

HATS

Types

baseball
top hat
hard hat
bonnet
stocking cap
ski hat
cowboy hat
sombrero
helmet
hood
derby
graduation
birthday
yarmulka
headdresses
veils
turbans

Materials

felt
plastic
canvas
wool
fur
yarn
leather

Parts

crown
brim

Theme Goals:

Through participating in the experiences provided by this theme, the children may learn:

1. Types of hats.

2. Uses for hats.

3. Materials used to make hats.

4. Parts of a hat.

5. Colors and sizes of hats.

Concepts for the Children to Learn:

1. Hats are worn on our heads.

2. Some hats keep us warm.

3. Felt, plastic, cloth, and yarn are all materials used to make hats.

4. Hats come in different sizes.

5. Hats come in different colors.

6. Some hats have special names.

7. Some hats can keep us cool.

8. Hats can be worn for fun.

9. Some people wear hats when they are working.

10. Most hats have a crown and a brim.

Vocabulary:

1. **hat**—a covering for the head.

2. **crown**—top part of the hat.

3. **brim**—the part of a hat that surrounds the crown.

Bulletin Board

The purpose of this bulletin board is to have the children match the colored pieces to their corresponding shadow, thereby developing visual discrimination skills. To construct the bulletin board, draw different types of hats on white tagboard. Color the hats with watercolor markers and cut out. Trace the cut-out hats onto black construction paper to create shadows. Then cut the shadows out and attach to the bulletin board. A magnet piece or a push pin can be fastened to the shadow. A magnet piece or a hole can be applied to the colored hats.

Parent Letter

Dear Parents,

Hats will be the focus of our next curriculum. Through this unit the children will become familiar with occupations and sports for which hats are worn, materials used to make hats, and purposes of hats such as for protection, decoration, and identification.

At School

Some of the learning activities planned include:

- playing in the Hat Store located in the dramatic play area.
- making paper plate hats at the art table.
- listening to and dramatizing the story, *Caps for Sale*, by Esphyr Slobodkina.

Special Request!

On Friday we will have a Hat Day. The children will show and wear hats that they have brought from home. If your child wishes to share a special hat, please label it and send it to school with your child in a paper bag. This will help us to keep track of which hat belongs to each child. Thank you for your help.

At Home

Ask your child to help you search the closets of your home for hats. To develop classification skills, discuss the colors and types of hats with your child. Are there more seasonal hats or sports hats? What are the hats made from? Why were those materials used?

Hats off to a fun unit!

Hats serve many different functions and represent many different areas of the world.

Magnifying glasses can also be provided to allow the children to explore. They can look at, feel, and try on the hats.

- Before letting the children try on the hats, make sure the children do not have head lice.

Dramatic Play:

1. **Sports Hats**

   Provide football helmets and jerseys, baseball hats, batters' helmets, and uniforms. Encourage the children to pretend they are football and baseball players.

2. **Construction Site**

   Provide the children with toy tools, blocks, and construction hard hats.

3. **Hat Store**

   Fire fighter hats, bonnets, top hats, hard hats, bridesmaids' hats, baby hats, etc., can all be available in the hat store. Encourage the children to buy and sell hats using a cash register and play money.

Music:

"My Hat"
  (traditional song)

  My hat it has three corners.
    (point to head, hold up three fingers)
  Three corners has my hat.
    (hold up three fingers, point to head)
  And had it not three corners
    (hold up three fingers)
  It wouldn't be my hat.
    (shake head, point to head)

Variation: Make three-cornered paper hats to wear while acting out this song.

Arts and Crafts:

1. **Easel Ideas**

   - top hat-shaped paper
   - baseball cap-shaped paper
   - football helmet-shaped paper
   - graduation cap-shaped paper

2. **Paper Plate Hats**

   Decorate paper plates with many different kinds of scraps, glitter, construction paper, and crepe paper. Punch a hole, using a paper punch, on each side of the hat. Attach strings so that the hat can be tied on and fastened under the chin.

Science:

What's It Made Of?

Hats representing a variety of styles and materials can be placed on the science table.

Large Muscle:

Hat Bean Bag Toss

Lay several large hats on the floor. Encourage the children to stand about two feet from the hats and try to throw the beanbags into the hats.

Field Trips:

1. **Hat Store**

   Visit a hat store or hat department of a store. Examine the different kinds, sizes, and colors of hats.

2. **Sports Store**

   Visit a sporting goods store. Locate the hat section. Observe the types of hats used for different sports.

Math:

1. **Hat Match**

   Construct pairs of hat puzzles out of tagboard. On each pair, draw a different pattern. Encourage the children to mix the hats up and sort them by design.

2. **Hat Seriation**

   Collect a variety of hats. The children can arrange them from smallest to largest and largest to smallest. Also, they can classify the hats by colors and uses.

Social Studies:

Many of these activities lend themselves to group time situations.

1. **"Weather" or Not to Wear a Hat**

   Discuss the different kinds of hats that are worn in cold weather. Ask questions such as, "What parts of our body does a hat keep warm?" "What kind of hats do we wear when it is warm outside?" "How does a hat help to keep us cool?"

2. **Sports Hats**

   Make an arrangement of different sports hats. Place a mirror close by. The children can try on the hats.

3. **Community Helpers**

   Many people in our community wear hats as part of their uniform. Collect several of these hats such as fire fighter, police officer, mail carrier, baker, etc., and place in a bag for a small group activity. Identify one child at a time to pull a hat out of the bag. Once the hat is removed, the children can identify the worker. Older children may be able to describe the activities of the identified worker.

Group Time (games, language):

1. **"My Favorite Hat Day"**

   Encourage the children to share their favorite hats with the class on a specific day. Talk about each hat and ask where it was bought or found. Colors, sizes, and shapes can also be discussed.

2. **Dramatization**

   Read the story, *Caps for Sale*. After the children are familiar with the storyline, they may enjoy acting out the story.

Cooking:

The children may enjoy wearing baker's hats for the cooking experiences! Ask a bakery or fast-food restaurant to donate several for classroom use.

1. **Cheese Crunchies**

   1/2 cup butter or margarine
   1 cup all-purpose flour
   1 cup shredded cheddar cheese

pinch of salt
1 cup rice cereal bits

Cut the butter into 6 or 8 slices and mix together with the flour, cheese, and salt. Use fingers or fork to mix. Knead in the cereal bits; then roll the dough into small balls or snakes. Press them down flat and place onto an ungreased cookie sheet. Bake at 325 degrees for approximately 10 minutes. Cool and serve for snack.

2. **Hamantaschen from Israel**

Children in Israel eat hamantaschen on the holiday of Purim. A hamantaschen is a pastry that represents the hat worn by the evil Haman, who plotted against the ancient Jews. Today, Israeli children dress in costumes, parade in the streets, and have parties on Purim.

7 tablespoons butter or margarine
1/3 cup sugar

2 eggs
2 1/2 cups flour
1/4 cup orange juice
1 teaspoon lemon juice
1 jar prune or plum jam

Cream the butter or margarine and sugar together in a large mixing bowl. Separate the eggs. Discard the whites. Add the yolk to the mixture and stir. Add the flour and juices to the mixture and mix to form dough. On a floured board, roll the dough to about 1/8-inch thickness. Use a cookie cutter to cut into 4-inch circles. Spoon a tablespoon of jam into the center of each circle and fold up 3 edges to create a triangle shape. Leave a small opening at the center. (Other fillings, such as poppy seeds or apricot jam, can be used.) Place the shaped dough on a cookie sheet and bake for 20 minutes in a 350-degree preheated oven. Serve for snack.

HATS

A variety of hats can be collected for use in the dramatic play area. Some examples are:

fire fighter	railroad engineer	ski caps
police officer	motorcycle helmet	berets
visor	cloche	top hat
sunbonnets	sports:	cowboy
sombrero	football	stocking cap
straw hats	baseball	mail carrier
mantilla	chef	bicycle helmet
party (birthday)	sailor	pillbox
nurse's cap	hard hats	

Books:

The following books can be used to complement the theme:

1. Cooke, Tom (Illus.). (1987). *I Want a Hat Like That*. New York: Golden Press.

2. Geringer, Laura. (1987). *A Three Hat Day*. New York: Harper Collins.

3. Mark, Jan. (1986). *Fur*. New York: Harper and Row.

4. Schumacher, Claire. (1987). *Santa's Hat*. New York: Prentice Hall Books.

5. Morris, Ann. (1993). *Hats, Hats, Hats*. New York: Morrow.

6. Barkan, Joanne. (1992). *That Fat Hat*. New York: Scholastic Inc.

7. Cushman, Dough. (1988). *Uncle Foster's Hat Tree*. New York: Dutton Children's Books.

8. Hindley, Judy. (1991). *Uncle Harold and the Green Hat*. New York: Farrar, Straus and Girous.

9. Howard, Elizabeth F. (1991). *Aunt Flossie's Hats (and Crab Cakes Later)*. Boston: Houghton Mifflin.

10. Leemis, Ralph. (1991). *Mister Momboo's Hat*. New York: Dutton Children's Books.

11. Miller, Margaret. (1988). *Whose Hat?* New York: Greenwillow Books.

12. Scarry, Richard. (1990). *Be Careful! Mr. Fumble!* New York: Random House Books for Young Readers.

13. Walbrecker, Dirk. (1991). *Benny's Hat*. Wilmington, DE: Atonium Books, Inc.

14. Borden, Louise. (1989). *Caps, Hats, Socks, and Mittens*. New York: Scholastic.

15. Roy, Ron. (1987). *Whose Hat Is That?* Boston: Houghton Mifflin.

16. Schneider, Howie. (1993). *Uncle Lester's Hat*. New York: Putnam.

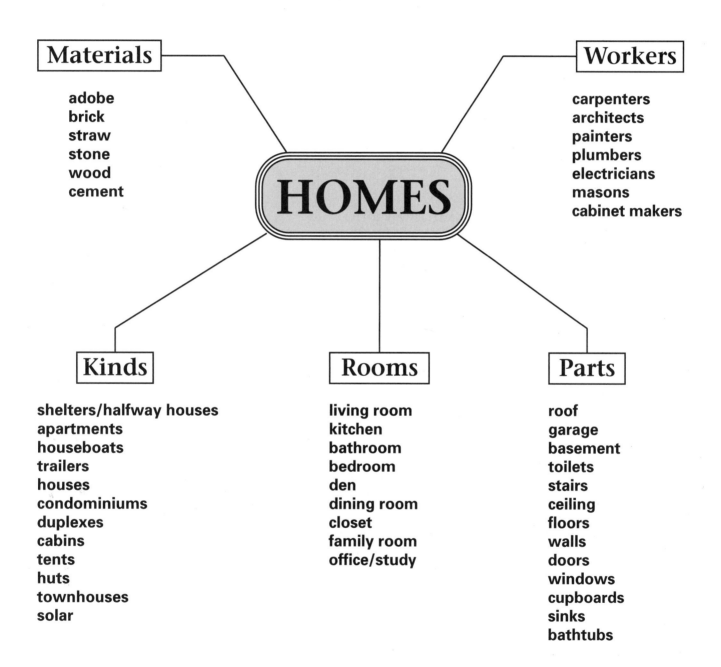

Materials

adobe
brick
straw
stone
wood
cement

Workers

carpenters
architects
painters
plumbers
electricians
masons
cabinet makers

HOMES

Kinds

shelters/halfway houses
apartments
houseboats
trailers
houses
condominiums
duplexes
cabins
tents
huts
townhouses
solar

Rooms

living room
kitchen
bathroom
bedroom
den
dining room
closet
family room
office/study

Parts

roof
garage
basement
toilets
stairs
ceiling
floors
walls
doors
windows
cupboards
sinks
bathtubs

Theme Goals:

Through participating in the experiences provided by this theme, the children may learn about:

1. Home builders.

2. Parts of a home.

3. Rooms in a home.

4. Kinds of homes.

5. Building materials.

Concepts for the Children to Learn:

1. A home is a place to live.

2. Apartments, condominiums, trailers, and houses are all kinds of homes.

3. Most homes have a kitchen, bedroom, bathroom, and living room.

4. Homes can be built from brick, stone, wood, or cement.

5. The ceiling, floor, roof, and windows are parts of a home.

6. Construction workers build houses.

7. Homes come in many sizes.

8. Homes can be decorated many ways.

Vocabulary:

1. **apartment**—a building including many homes.

2. **duplex**—a house divided into two separate homes.

3. **house**—a place to live.

4. **construction worker**—a person who builds.

5. **kitchen**—a room for cooking.

6. **bedroom**—a room for sleeping.

7. **architect**—a person who designs homes.

Bulletin Board

The purpose of this bulletin board is to develop classification skills. Draw an unfurnished model of a home on a large sheet of tagboard as illustrated. Include the basic rooms such as kitchen, bedroom, and living room. Draw and cut furnishings to add to the home. Laminate home and furnishings. The children can place the furnishings in the proper room by using "fun tack" or magnetic strips on the furnishings.

Parent Letter

Dear Parents,

Homes will be the focus of our next curricular theme. Since everyone's home is unique we will be discussing how homes differ. We will also be discussing activities we do in our home and the rooms in our homes.

At School

Some of our activities will include:

- constructing homes out of cardboard boxes and paper in the art area.
- acting out the story of *The Three Little Pigs* in the dramatic play area.
- building at the workbench.

A special activity will include making placemats, but we need your help. For our placemats we will need a few pictures of your family, home, or both. These will be glued to construction paper and laminated during our project. They will not be returned in their original form. Thank you!

This week we will also be taking a neighborhood tour to observe the various types of homes in the area. We will be taking our walk at 10:00 a.m. on Thursday. Please feel free to join us!

At Home

To develop observation skills, take your child on a walk around your neighborhood to look at the houses in your area. Talk about the different colors and sizes of dwellings.

Enjoy the time you spend with your child!

Playing house is an activity that builds interpersonal skills.

Music:

"This is the Way We Build Our House"
(Sing to the tune of "Here We Go 'Round the Mulberry Bush")

This is the way we build our house
So early in the morning.

Other suggestions:
This is the way we paint the house.
This is the way we wash the car.
This is the way we rake the leaves.

Fingerplays:

MY HOUSE

I'm going to build a little house
(fingers make roof)
With windows big and bright
(stand with arms in air)
Drifting out of sight.
In winter when the snowflakes fall
(hands flutter down)

Or when I hear a storm
(hand cupped to ear)
I'll go sit in my little house
(sit down)
Where I'll be snug and warm.
(cross arms over chest)

WHERE SHOULD I LIVE?

Where should I live?
In a castle with towers and a moat?
(make a point with arms over head)
Or on a river in a houseboat?
(make wave like motions)
A winter igloo made of ice may be just the thing
(pretend to pack snow)
But what would happen when it turned to spring?
(pretend to think)
I like tall apartments and houses made of stone,
(stretch up tall)
But I'd also like to live in a blue mobile home.
(shorten up)
A cave or cabin in the woods would give me lots of space
(stretch out wide)
But I guess my home is the best place!
(point to self)

KNOCKING

Look at _____ knocking on our door.
   (knock)
Look at _____ knocking on our door.
   (knock)
Come on in out of the cold
   (shiver)
Into our nice, warm home.
   (rub hands together to be warm)

MY CHORES

In my home, I wash the dishes
   (pretend to wash)
Vacuum the floor
   (push vacuum)
And dust the furniture.
   (dust)
Outside my home, I rake the leaves
   (rake)
Plant the flowers
   (plant)
And play hard all day.
   (wipe sweat from forehead)
When the day is over
I eat my supper,
   (eat)
Read a story
   (read)
And go to sleep.
   (put head on hands)

Science:

Building Materials

Building materials with magnifying glasses should be placed in the science area. The children may observe and examine materials. Included may be wood, brick, canvas, tar paper, shingles, etc.

Dramatic Play:

1. **Tent Living**

   A small tent can be set up indoors or outdoors depending upon weather and space. Accessories such as sleeping bags, flashlights, rope, cooking utensils, and backpacks should also be provided if available.

2. **Cardboard Houses**

   Collect large cardboard boxes. Place outdoors or in an open classroom area. The children may build their own homes. If desired, tempera paint can be used for painting the homes. Wallpaper may also be provided.

3. **Cleaning House**

   Housecleaning tools such as a vacuum cleaner, dusting cloth, sponges, mops, and brooms can be placed in the dramatic play area. During the self-selected play periods the children may choose to participate in cleaning.

Arts and Crafts:

1. **Shape Homes**

   An assortment of construction paper shapes such as squares, triangles, rectangles, and circles should be placed on a table in the art area. Glue and large pieces of paper should also be provided.

2. **Tile Painting**

   Ask building companies to donate cracked, chipped, or discontinued tiles. The children can paint tiles.

3. **Homes I Like**

   The children can cut pictures of homes, rooms, appliances, and furniture from magazines. They can glue these pieces on large construction paper pieces. The construction paper can be stapled. A cover can also be added and labeled, "Things in My Home."

4. **Household Tracings**

   Several household items such as a spatula, wooden spoon, pizza cutter, or cookie cutter can be placed on the art table. Also include paper, scissors, and crayons. These items can be traced. Some of the older children may color and cut their tracings.

Sensory:

1. Identifying Sounds

Record several sounds found in the home such as a vacuum cleaner, television, water running, and a toilet flushing. Encourage children to name sounds. For older children, this could also be played as a lotto game. Make cards containing pictures of sounds; vary pictures from card to card. When a sound is heard, cover the corresponding picture with a chip.

2. Sand Castles

Add wet sand to the sensory table. Provide forms to create buildings, homes, etc. Examples may include empty cans, milk cartons, plastic containers, etc.

Large Muscle:

Pounding Nails

Collect building materials such as soft pine scraps and styrofoam for the workbench. Adult supervision is always required with this activity.

Field Trips/Resource People:

1. Neighborhood Walk

Walk around the neighborhood. Observe the construction workers' actions and tools.

2. Construction Site

If available visit a local construction site. Discuss the role of the construction worker.

3. Resource People

The following resource people could be invited to the classroom:

- builder
- architect
- plumber
- painter
- electrician

Math:

My House

Construct a "My House" book for each child. On the pages write things like:

"My home has _____ steps."
My home is the color _____.
My home has _____ windows.
There are _____ doors in my home.
My home has _____ keyholes.

Other ideas could include the number of beds, people, pets, etc. Send this home with the child to complete with parents.

Social Studies:

Room Match

Collect several boxes. On one box print kitchen; on another print bathroom; on another print living room; and on another print bedroom. Then cut objects related to each of these rooms from catalogs. The children may sort objects by placing them in the appropriate boxes. To illustrate, dishes, silverware, and a coffee pot would be placed in the box labeled kitchen.

Group Time (games, language):

Construct a "My home is special because…" chart. Encourage the children to name a special thing about their homes. Display the chart at the children's eye level in the classroom for the week.

Cooking:

Individual Pizza

English muffins
pizza sauce
grated mozzarella cheese

Spread a tablespoon of sauce on each muffin half. Sprinkle the top with grated cheese. Bake in a preheated oven at 375 degrees until cheese melts.

Multimedia:

The following resources can be found in educational catalogs:

1. Seeger, Pete. *American Folk Songs for Children* [record]. Folkway Records.

2. Rogers, Fred. *A Place of Our Own* [record]. Dickwick International, Inc.

3. Jenkins, Ella. *My Street Begins at My House* [record].

4. *Fisher-Price Classics* [Apple/IBM software, PK–1]. Gametek.

5. *Early Learning* [IBM/Mac/Apple software, PK–2]. Compu-Tech.

6. *Early Games* [Apple/IBM software, PK–1]. Queue.

Books:

The following books can be used to complement the theme:

1. North, Carol. (1985). *The House Book.* Racine, WI: Western Publishing Company, Inc.

2. Durham, Robert. (1987). *Around the House.* Chicago: Children's Press.

3. Dorros, Arthur. (1992). *This Is My House.* New York: Scholastic, Inc.

4. Brown, Richard (Illus.). (1989). *One Hundred Words About My House.* San Diego: Harcourt Brace Jovanovich.

5. Emberly, Rebecca. (1990). *My House, Mi Casa: A Book in Two Languages.* New York: Little Brown and Co.

6. Gibbons, Gail. (1990). *How a House Is Built.* New York: Holiday House, Inc.

7. Ackerman, Karen. (1992). *This Old House.* New York: Macmillan Children's Book Group.

8. Hoberman, Mary A. (1982). *A House Is a House for Me.* New York: Puffin Books.

9. Rockwell, Anne. (1991). *In Our House.* New York: Harper Collins Children's Books.

10. Ringgold, Faith. (1991). *Tar Beach.* New York: Crown Publishers.

11. Wagon, Crescent Dragon. (1990). *Home Place.* New York: Macmillan.

12. Rosen, Michael J. (Ed.). (1992). *Home: A Collaboration.* New York: Harper Collins.

13. Barton, Byron. (1990). *Building a House.* New York: Morrow.

14. Brown, Margaret Wise. (1989). *Big Red Barn.* New York: Harper & Row.

15. Bowden, Jane. (1992). *Where Does Our Garbage Go?* New York: Bantam Doubleday Dell Publishing.

16. Kuklin, Susan. (1992). *How My Family Lives in America.* New York: Bradbury Press.

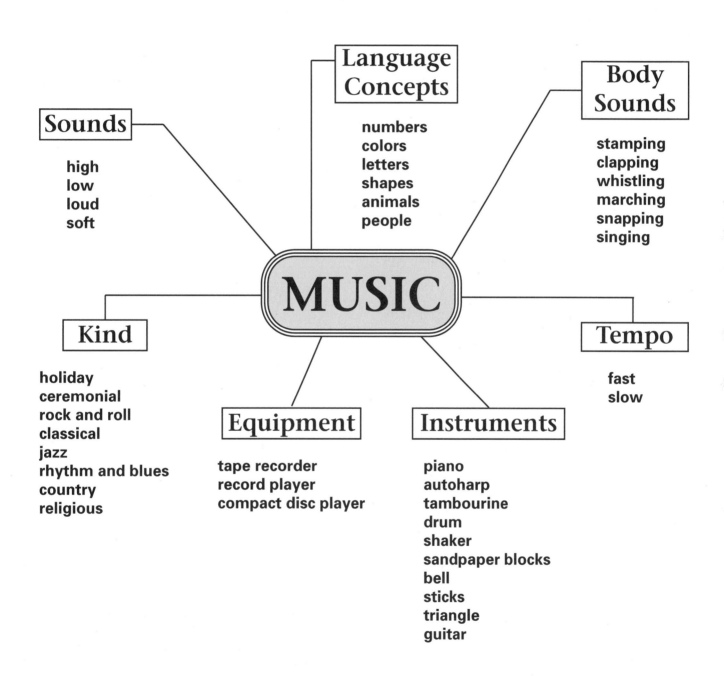

Language Concepts

numbers
colors
letters
shapes
animals
people

Body Sounds

stamping
clapping
whistling
marching
snapping
singing

Sounds

high
low
loud
soft

MUSIC

Kind

holiday
ceremonial
rock and roll
classical
jazz
rhythm and blues
country
religious

Tempo

fast
slow

Equipment

tape recorder
record player
compact disc player

Instruments

piano
autoharp
tambourine
drum
shaker
sandpaper blocks
bell
sticks
triangle
guitar

Theme Goals:

Through participating in the experiences provided by this theme, the children may learn:

1. Music is a language.
2. Kinds of music.
3. Music tempos.
4. Language concepts.
5. Different sounds.
6. Names of many musical instruments.
7. Body sounds.
8. Equipment used for playing and recording music.

Concepts for the Children to Learn:

1. There are many types of instruments.
2. Each instrument has its own sound.
3. Music sounds can be high, low, loud, and soft.
4. Music can express different moods.
5. Music can be played in different rhythms.
6. Songs can tell stories.
7. Our bodies are musical instruments.
8. Our hands can clap.
9. Our feet can stamp and march.
10. Our fingers can snap.
11. Our mouths can whistle and sing.
12. The piano, autoharp, and guitar are played with our fingers.
13. Sticks are used on the triangle, drum, xylophone, and bells.
14. We shake bells, shakers, and tambourines.
15. We rub sandpaper blocks.
16. There are many kinds of music.
17. We can tape music with a recorder.
18. A record, tape, or compact disc player can play music.

Vocabulary:

1. **music**—a way of expressing ideas and feelings.
2. **instrument**—makes musical sounds.
3. **tempo**—the speed of music.
4. **body sounds**—sounds made by moving one or more body parts.
5. **mallets**—special sticks used to play the xylophone and bells.

Bulletin Board

The purpose of this bulletin board is to develop visual discrimination skills. Create a musical bulletin board by drawing musical instruments on tagboard as illustrated. Color the instruments with markers, cut out, and laminate. Trace these pieces onto black construction paper. Cut out the pieces and attach to the bulletin board. A magnet should be attached to both the colored pieces and the black shadow pieces. The children can match the appropriately shaped instrument piece to its shadow on the bulletin board.

Parent Letter

Dear Parents,

We will be singing and playing instruments during our unit on music. Music is a way of communicating and expressing oneself. For young children, singing is not that much different from talking—as I'm sure you've noticed from observing the children! Throughout the unit the children will be making discoveries about the many sounds that we can make with our voices, body parts, and musical instruments.

At School

A few highlights of our scheduled musical learning activities include:

- making musical instruments.
- painting at the easel while listening to music with headphones.
- trying on band uniforms (courtesy of Mead School) in the dramatic play area.
- forming a rhythm band outside in the play yard.

At Home

To stimulate creativity and language, create verses with your child for this song to the tune of "Old McDonald Had A Farm:"

Mr. Roberts had a band,
E-I-E-I-O.
And in his band he had a drum
E-I-E-I-O.
With a boom, boom, here, and a boom, boom, there,
Here a boom, there a boom,
Everywhere a boom, boom.
Mr. Roberts had a band,
E-I-E-I-O.

And in his band he had a horn…
Continue adding instruments that your child can think of.

Provide materials for your child to make simple musical instruments. A drum can be made using an empty oatmeal carton or coffee can. Your child can personalize the instrument by decorating the outside of the container with paper, crayons, and markers. A kazoo can also be made with a cardboard tube and a small piece of waxed paper attached to the end of the tube with a rubber band. Poke a small hole in the waxed paper and your child will be ready to blow up a storm! The sounds produced by the different instruments can be compared to develop auditory discrimination skills.

Keep a song in your heart!

Children enjoy listening to and creating their own music.

Music:

Music for this unit should consist of the children's favorite and well-known songs. The children will enjoy singing these songs, and you will be able to focus on the sound of the music. Here are some suggestions of traditional songs that most children enjoy:

1. **"Old MacDonald Had a Farm"**

2. **"Five Green Speckled Frogs"**

3. **"The Farmer in the Dell"**

4. **"Row, Row, Row Your Boat"**

5. **"Mary Had a Little Lamb"**

6. **"Hickory Dickory Dock"**

7. **"If You're Happy and You Know It"**

8. **"ABC Song"**

9. **"The Little White Duck"**

10. **"Six Little Ducks"**

Fingerplays:

I WANT TO LEAD A BAND

I want to lead a band
With a baton in my hand.
   (wave baton in air)
I want to make sweet music high and low.
Now first I'll beat the drum
   (drum-beating motion)
With a rhythmic tum-tum-tum,
And then I'll play the bells
A-ting-a-ling-a ling,
   (bell-playing motion)
And next I'll blow the flute
With a cheery toot-a-toot.
   (flute-playing motion)
Then I'll make the violin sweetly sing.
   (violin-playing motion)
Now I'm leading a band
With a baton in my hand.
   (wave baton in air again)

IF I COULD PLAY

If I could play the piano
This is the way I would play.
   (move fingers like playing a piano)

If I had a guitar
I would strum the strings this way.
   (hold guitar and strum)

If I had a trumpet
I'd toot to make a tune.
   (play trumpet)

But if I had a drum
I'd go boom, boom, boom.
   (pretend to play a drum)

MUSICAL INSTRUMENTS

This is how a horn sounds
Toot! Toot! Toot!
   (play imaginary horn)

This is how guitars sound
Vrrroom, Vrrroom, Vrrroom
   (strum imaginary guitar)

This is how the piano sounds
Tinkle, grumble, brring.
   (run fingers over imaginary keyboard)

This is how the drum sounds
Rat-a-tat, grumble, brring.
   (strike drum, include cymbal)

JACK-IN-THE-BOX

Jack-in-the-box all shut up tight
   (fingers wrapped around thumb)
Not a breath of air, not a ray of light.
   (other hand covers fist)
How tired he must be all down in a heap.
   (lift off)
I'll open the lid and up he will leap!
   (thumbs pop out)

Science:

1. **Water Music**

   Fill four identically sized crystal glasses each
   with a different amount of water. The children
   can trace their wet finger around the rim of
   each glass. Each glass will have a different
   tune. Older children may enjoy reordering the
   glasses from the highest to the lowest tone.

2. **Pop Bottle Music**

   Fill six 12-ounce pop bottles, each with a
   different amount of water. For effect, in each
   bottle place a drop of food coloring, providing
   six different colors. Younger children can tap
   the bottles with a spoon as they listen for the
   sound. Older children may try blowing
   directly into the opening for sound production.

3. **Throats**

   Show the children how to place their hands
   across their throat. Then have them whisper,
   talk, shout, and sing feeling the differences in
   vibration.

4. **Jumping Seeds**

   Set seeds or something small on top of a drum.
   Then beat the drum. What happens? Why?
   This activity can be extended by having the
   childen jump to the drum beat.

5. **Identifying Instruments**

   Prepare a tape recording of classroom musical
   instruments. Play the tape, encouraging the
   children to identify the correct instrument
   related to each sound.

6. **Matching Sounds**

   Collect 12 containers, such as film canisters,
   milk cartons, or covered baby food jars, that
   would be safe to use with the children. Fill 2
   containers with rice, 2 cans with beans, 2 cans
   with pebbles, 2 cans with water, and the
   remaining cans with dry pasta. Coins, such as
   pennies, could be substituted. Color code each
   pair of containers on the bottom. Let the
   children shake the containers, listening to the
   sounds, in an attempt to find the matching
   pairs.

Dramatic Play:

1. **Band**

   Collect materials for a band prop box, which
   may include band uniforms, a baton, music
   stand, cassette player, and tapes with marching
   music. The children can experiment with
   instruments.

2. Dramatizing

Add a cassette recorder and a small microphone to the dramatic play area. The children may enjoy using it for singing and recording their voices.

3. Disc Jockey

In the music area, provide a tape recorder and cassettes for the children.

Arts and Crafts:

1. Drums

Create drums out of empty coffee cans with plastic lids, plastic ice cream pails, or oatmeal boxes. The children can decorate as desired with paper, paint, felt-tip markers, or crayons.

2. Shakers

Collect a variety of egg-shaped panty hose containers. Fill each egg with varying amounts of sand, peas, or rice, and securely tape or glue them shut. To compare sounds, empty film containers can also be filled.

3. Cymbals

Make cymbals out of old tin foil pans. Attach a string for the handles.

4. Tambourines

Two paper plates can be made into a tambourine. Begin by placing pop bottle caps or small stones between the plates. Staple the paper plates together. Shake to produce sound.

5. Easel Ideas

Cut easel paper into the shape of different instruments such as a drum, guitar, or tambourine.

6. Musical Painting

On a table in the art area, place a tape recorder with headphones. The children can listen to music as they paint.

7. Kazoos

Kazoos can be made with empty paper towel rolls and waxed paper. The children can decorate the outside of the kazoos with colored felt-tip markers. After this, place a piece of waxed paper over one end of the roll and secure it with a rubber band. Poke two or three small holes into the waxed paper allowing sound to be produced.

8. Rhythm Sticks

Two wooden dowels should be given to each interested child. The sticks can be decorated with paint or colored felt-tip markers.

Large Muscle:

1. Body Movement Rhythms

Introduce a simple body movement. Then have the children repeat it until they develop a rhythm. Examples include:

- stamp foot, clap hands, stamp foot, clap hands
- clap, clap, stamp, stamp
- clap, stamp, clap, stamp
- clap, clap, snap fingers
- clap, snap, stamp, clap, snap, stamp
- clap, clap, stamp, clap, clap, stamp

2. Body Percussion

Instruct the children to stand in a circle. Repeat the following rhythmic speech:

We walk and we walk and we stop (rest)
We walk and we walk and we stop (rest)
We walk and we walk and we walk and we walk
We walk and we walk and we stop. (stop)

3. March

Play different rhythm beats on a piano or another instrument. Examples include hopping, skipping, gliding, walking, running, tiptoeing, galloping, etc. The children can move to the rhythm.

Field Trips/Resource People:

1. **Band Director**

   Visit a school band director. Observe the different instruments available to students. Listen to their sounds.

2. **Who Can Play?**

   Invite parents, grandparents, brothers, sisters, relatives, friends, etc., to visit the classroom and demonstrate their talent.

3. **Radio Station**

   Visit a local radio station.

4. **Taping**

   Videotape the children singing and using rhythm instruments. Replay the video for the children. Save this for a future open house, parent meeting, or holiday celebration.

Math:

1. **Colors, Shapes, and Numbers**

   Sing the song, "Colors, Shapes, and Numbers," mentioned in the shapes unit or make up a song about shapes. Hold up different colors, shapes, and numbers while you sing the song for the children to identify.

2. **Number Rhyme**

   Say the following song to reinforce numbers:

   One, two, three, four
   Come right in and shut the door.
   Five, six, seven, eight
   Come right in. It's getting late.
   Nine, ten, eleven, twelve
   Put your books upon the shelves.
   Will you count along with me?
   It's as easy as can be!

3. **Ten in the Bed**

   Chant the following words to reinforce numbers:

There were 10 in the bed and the little one said, "Roll over, roll over."
So they all rolled over and one fell out.

There were 9 in the bed and the little one said, "Roll over, roll over."
So they all rolled over and one fell out.

Continue until there is only one left. The last line will be "…and the little one said, "Good night!""

4. **Music Calendar**

   Design a calendar for the month of your music unit. The different days of the week can be made out of musical notes and different instruments.

Social Studies:

1. **Our Own Songs**

   Encourage the children to help you write a song about a common class experience. Substitute the words into a melody that everyone knows ("Twinkle, Twinkle, Little Star" or "The Mulberry Bush").

2. **Pictures**

   Put up pictures of instruments and band players in the room to add interest and stimulate discussion.

3. **Sound Tapes**

   Make a special tape of sounds heard in a home. Homes are full of different sounds. Included may be:

   - people knocking on doors
   - wind chimes
   - telephone ringing
   - teakettle whistling
   - clock ticking
   - toilet flushing
   - popcorn popping
   - vacuum cleaner
   - doorbell
   - running water
   - car horn

Play the tape and have the children listen carefully to identify the sounds.

Group Time (games, language):

1. Name Game

Say the following rhythmic chant as the whole class claps.

"Names, names we all have names
Play a game as we say our names
Scott (class echoes) Scott
Melanie (class echoes) Melanie
Tommy (class echoes) Tommy."

Repeat until all the children have had their name repeated.

Source: *The Kinder-Music House*. (1982). Fairfax County Public Schools.

2. Are You Here?

Sing the following song to the tune of "Twinkle, Twinkle, Little Star."

Hello, children, here we are,
At our school from near and far.
Today we are going to play a game,
Please stand when I call your name.

Source: Beckman, Simmons, & Thomas. (1982). *Channels to Children*. Colorado: Channels to Children Publishing Company.

Miscellaneous:

Instrument of the Day

Focus on a different instrument each day. Talk about the construction and demonstrate the instrument's sound.

Cooking:

Popcorn

Make popcorn and have the children listen to the sounds of the oil as well as the corn popping. Supervise this activity closely since the corn popper will become hot. This activity is most appropriate for older children— younger children may choke on popcorn.

Multimedia:

The following resources can be found in educational catalogs:

1. *Simplified Lummi Stick Activities* [record]. Kimbo.

2. Palmer, Hap. *Getting to Know Myself* [record].

3. *Color Me a Rainbow* [record]. Melody House.

4. *Music Skills* [record]. Melody House.

5. "Scat Like That," *On the Move with Greg and Steve* [record]. Youngheart Records.

6. "Sing a Happy Song," *We All Live Together Series—Vol. 3* [record]. Youngheart Records.

7. *Family Folk Festival: A Multicultural Sing-Along* [record]. Scholastic.

8. *Rhythm Band Time* [record]. Melody House Records.

9. *Shake It to the One That You Love the Best: Play Songs and Lullabies from Black Musical Tradition* [record]. Mattox.

Books:

The following books can be used to complement the theme:

1. Lillegard, Dee. (1987). *Percussion*. Chicago: Children's Press.

2. Lillegard, Dee. (1987). *Woodwinds*. Chicago: Children's Press.

3. Raffi. (1987). *Down by the Bay*. New York: Crown Publishers.

4. Greenfield, Eloise. (1991). *I Make Music*. New York: Writers and Readers Publishing, Inc.

5. Gregorich, Barbara. (1991). *A Different Tune*. Grand Haven, MI: School Zone Publishing Co.

6. Keats, Ezra J. (1989). *Louie's Search*. New York: Macmillan Children's Book Group.

7. Komaiko, Leah. (1987). *I Like the Music*. New York: Harper Collins Children's Books.

8. Kraus, Robert. (1990). *Musical Max*. New York: Simon and Schuster Trade.

9. McCurdy, Michael. (1992). *The Old Man and the Fiddle*. New York: Putnam Publishing Group.

10. Micucci, Charles. (1989). *A Little Night Music*. New York: Morrow Junior Books.

11. Muntean, Michaela. (1991). *Grover's Overtunes*. Astor, FL: Astor Publications.

12. Rubin, Mark. (1992). *The Orchestra*. Buffalo, NY: Firefly Books, Ltd.

13. Sage, James. (1991). *The Little Band*. New York: Macmillan Children's Book Group.

14. Sharmat, Marjorie W. (1991). *Nate the Great and the Musical Note*. New York: Dell Publishing Co., Inc.

15. Lillegard, Dee. (1989). *Brass*. Chicago: Children's Press.

16. Lillegard, Dee. (1988). *Strings*. Chicago: Children's Press.

17. Williams, Vera B. (1989). *Music, Music for Everyone*. New York: Morrow.

18. Ziefert, Harriet. (1992). *Music Lessons*. New York: Harper Collins.

19. Kherdian, David, & Hogrogian, Nonny. (1990). *The Cat's Midsummer Jamboree*. New York: Philomel.

20. Medearis, Angela S. (1992). *The Zebra-Riding Cowboy: A Folk Song From the Old West*. New York: Henry Holt & Co.

21. Hart, Avery, & Mantell, Paul. (1993). *Kids Make Music! Clapping & Tapping from Bach to Rock*. Charlotte, VT: Williamstown.

22. Weil, Lisl. (1989). *The Magic of Music*. New York: Holiday.

23. Hart, Jane (Ed.). (1989). *Singing Bee!: A Collection of Favorite Children's Songs*. New York: Lothrop, Lee, & Shepard.

24. Ackerman, Karen. (1988). *Song and Dance Man*. New York: Alfred A. Knopf.

25. deRegniers, Beatrice Schenk (Ed.). (1988). *Sing a Song of Popcorn: Every Child's Book of Poems*. New York: Scholastic.

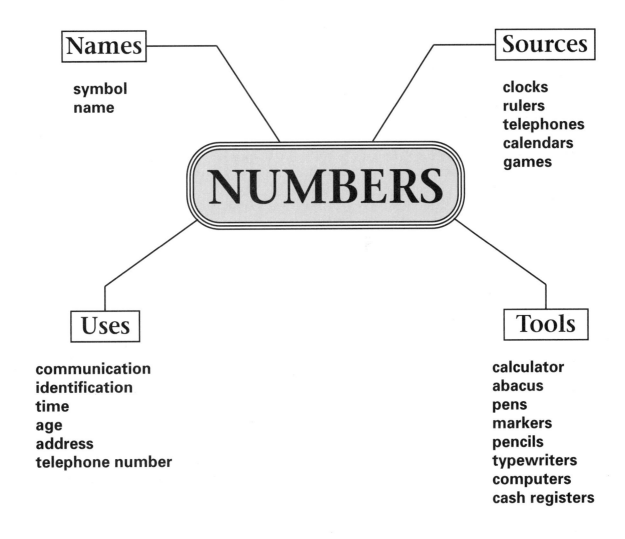

Names

symbol
name

Sources

clocks
rulers
telephones
calendars
games

NUMBERS

Uses

communication
identification
time
age
address
telephone number

Tools

calculator
abacus
pens
markers
pencils
typewriters
computers
cash registers

Theme Goals:

Through participating in the experiences provided by this theme, the children may learn:

1. Uses of numbers.

2. Sources of numbers.

3. Number names.

4. Tools for recording numbers.

Concepts for the Children to Learn:

1. A number is a symbol.

2. Each number symbol has a name.

3. Pencils, typewriters, and computers are tools used to make numbers.

4. Numbers can be found on clocks, rulers, telephones, and calendars.

5. Communication, identification, time, and age are uses for numbers.

6. Adding machines and cash registers have numerals.

Vocabulary:

1. **numeral**—a symbol that represents a number.

2. **number**—a symbol used to represent an amount.

Bulletin Board

The objective of this bulletin board is for the children to match the numeral to the set by winding the string around the other push pin. Construct the numerals out of tagboard. Construct objects familiar to the child to correspond to one type of object to each numeral. The number of objects and numerals should be developmentally appropriate for the group of children. Laminate. Staple 1, 2, 3, 4, and 5 down the left side of bulletin board. Staple the sets of objects in random order (3, 5, 1, 2, 4) down the right side of the bulletin board as illustrated. Affix a push pin with an attached long string by each numeral. Affix a push pin in front of each set row.

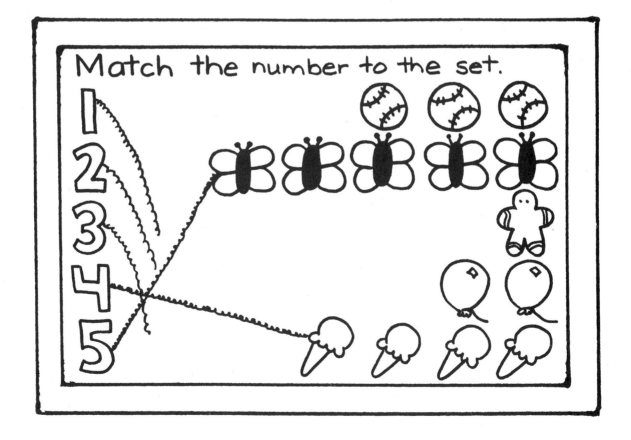

Parent Letter

Dear Parents,

Our next unit will focus on numbers. The children will be exposed to concepts of pairs, sets, and halves and wholes. They will also be participating in activities that include the concepts of heavy/light, bigger/smaller, and more/less.

At School

Some of the play-related activities include:

- measuring with scales and rulers at the science table.
- charting our weight and height.
- listening to the book titled, *I Can Count*, by Lynn Grundy.
- using number cookie cutters with playdough.
- bowling with numbered pins.

Personnel from the telephone company will be visiting us Tuesday. They will show us a variety of phones. They will also stress the importance of knowing our telephone number. Feel free to join us for this activity.

At Home

Cooking provides a concrete foundation for mathematical concepts. It involves amounts, fractions, and measures. While you are cooking, have your child help. Count how many spoonfuls it takes to fill a one-cup measurer.

Your child can help you make this simple no-bake recipe for peanut butter treats.

Peanut Butter Treats

1/4 cup margarine
1/4 cup peanut butter
1 cup raisins
40 regular-size marshmallows
5 cups rice cereal

Melt margarine over low heat. Add marshmallows and melt. Add the peanut butter and stir. Add the rice cereal and raisins; stir until everything is mixed well. Spread the mixture into a buttered pan and press into a firm layer. Cool and cut into squares.

Enjoy counting with your child.

Developmentally appropriate software can be an effective strategy for teaching children numbers.

Music:

1. **"Hickory Dickory Dock"**
   (traditional)

   Hickory dickory dock.
   The mouse ran up the clock.
   The clock struck one,
   The mouse ran down.
   Hickory dickory dock.

2. **"Two Little Blackbirds"**
   (traditional)

   Two little blackbirds sitting on a hill
   One named Jack,
   One named Jill.
   Fly away, Jack,
   Fly away, Jill.
   Come back, Jack,
   Come back, Jill.
   Two little blackbirds sitting on a hill
   One named Jack,
   One named Jill.

Fingerplays:

I CAN EVEN COUNT SOME MORE

One, two, three, four
I can even count some more.
Five, six, seven, eight
All my fingers stand up straight
Nine, ten are my thumb men.

FIVE LITTLE MONKEYS SWINGING FROM THE TREE

Five little monkeys swinging from the tree
Teasing Mr. Alligator, "You can't catch me."
Along comes Mr. Alligator as sneaky as can be
SNAP
4 little monkeys swinging from the tree.
3 little monkeys swinging from the tree.
2 little monkeys swinging from the tree.
1 little monkey swinging from the tree.
No more monkeys swinging from the tree!

ONE, TWO, THREE

1, 2 How do you do?
1, 2, 3 Clap with me.
1, 2, 3, 4 Jump on the floor.

1, 2, 3, 4, 5 Look bright and alive!
1, 2, 3, 4, 5, 6 Pick up your sticks.
1, 2, 3, 4, 5, 6, 7 We can count up to eleven.
1, 2, 3, 4, 5, 6, 7, 8 Draw a circle around your plate.
1, 2, 3, 4, 5, 6, 7, 8, 9 Get the trunks in the line.
1, 2, 3, 4, 5, 6, 7, 8, 9, 10 Let's do it over again.

Source: Wilmes, Liz & Dick. (1983). *Everyday Circle Times*. Elgin, IL: Building Blocks Publications.

FIVE LITTLE BIRDS

Five little birds without any home.
　　(hold up five fingers)
Five little trees in a row.
　　(raise hands high over head)
Come build your nests in our branches tall.
　　(cup hands)
We'll rock them to and fro.

TEN LITTLE FINGERS

I have 10 little fingers and 10 little toes.
　　(children point to portions of body as they
　　repeat words)
Two little arms and one little nose.
One little mouth and two little ears.
Two little eyes for smiles and tears.
One little head and two little feet.
One little chin, that makes _____ complete.

Science:

1. **Height and Weight Chart**

   Design a height and weight chart for the classroom. The children can help by measuring each other. Record the numbers. Later in the year measure the children and record their progress. Note the differences.

2. **Using a Scale**

   Collect a variety of small objects and place on the science table with a balancing scale. The children can measure with the scale, noting the differences.

3. **Temperature**

   Place an outdoor thermometer on the playground. Encourage the children to examine the thermometer. Record the temperature. Mark the temperature on the thermometer with masking tape. Bring the thermometer into the classroom. Check the thermometer again in half an hour. Show the children the change in temperature.

Dramatic Play:

1. **Grocery Store**

   In the dramatic play area, arrange a grocery store. To do this, collect a variety of empty boxes, paper bags, sales receipts, etc. Removable stickers can be used to indicate the grocery prices. A cash register and play money can also be added to create interest.

2. **Clock Shop**

   Collect a variety of clocks for the children to explore. Using discarded clocks, with the glass face removed, is an interesting way to let the children explore numerals and internal mechanisms.

3. **Telephoning**

   Prepare a classroom telephone book with all the children's names and telephone numbers. Contact your local telephone company to borrow the training system. The children can practice dialing their own numbers as well as their classmates'.

Arts and Crafts:

1. **Marker Sets**

   Using rubber bands, bind two watercolor markers together. Repeat this procedure making several sets. Set the markers, including an unbound set, on the art table. The children can use the bound marker sets for creating designs on paper.

2. **Clipping Coupons**

   Collect coupon flyers from the Sunday edition of the paper and magazines for this activity. Place the flyers with scissors on a table in the art area. If interested, the children can cut coupons from the paper.

3. Coupon Collage

Clipped coupons, paste, and paper can be placed on a table in the art area.

4. Ruler Design

Collect a variety of rulers that are of different colors, sizes, and types. Using paper and a marking tool, the children can create designs.

5. Numeral Cookie Cutter

Numeral cookie cutters should be provided with playdough.

Sensory:

Add to the sensory table colored water and a variety of measuring tools.

Math:

1. Number Chain

Cut enough strips of paper to make a number chain for the days of the month. During group time each day, add a link to represent the passage of time. Another option is to use the chain as a countdown by removing a link per day until a special day. This is an interesting approach to an upcoming holiday.

2. Silverware Set

Provide a silverware set. The children can sort the pieces according to sizes, shapes, and/or use.

3. Constructing Numerals

Provide each interested child with a ball of play-dough. Instruct children to form some numerals randomly. It is important for the teacher to monitor work and correct reversals. Then children can add the proper corresponding number of dots for that numeral just formed.

An extension of this activity would be to make cards with numerals. The children roll their playdough into long ropes that could be placed over the lines of the numerals.

Group Time (games, language):

1. Squirrels in the Park

Choose five children to be squirrels. The children should sit in a row while one child pretends to go for a walk in the park carrying a bag of peanuts. When the child who is walking approaches the squirrels, provide directions. These may include: feeding the first squirrel, the fifth, the third, etc.

2. Block Form Board

On a large piece of cardboard trace around one of each of the shapes of the blocks in the block area. Let children match blocks to the shape on the board.

3. Match Them

Show the child several sets of identical picture cards, squares, objects, or flannel board pictures. Mix the items. Then have the children find matching pairs. One method of doing this is to hold up one item and have the children find the matching one.

4. Follow the Teacher

At group time, provide directions containing a number. For examples say 1 jump, 2 hops, 3 leaps, 4 tiptoe steps, etc. The numbers used should be developmentally appropriate for the children.

Cooking:

Peanut Butter Treats

1/4 cup margarine
1/4 cup peanut butter
1 cup raisins
40 regular-size marshmallows
5 cups rice cereal

Melt the margarine over low heat. Add marshmallows and melt. Add the peanut butter and stir. Add the rice cereal and raisins. Stir until all ingredients are well mixed. Spread the mixture onto a buttered pan and press into a firm layer. Let cool and cut into squares.

MANIPULATIVES FOR MATH ACTIVITIES

buttons
beads
bobbins
craft pompoms
spools
shells
seeds (corn, soybeans)
shelled peanuts
toothpicks
pennies

checkers
crayons
golf tees
plastic caps from markers,
    milk containers, plastic
    bottles
stickers
fishing bobbers
keys

small toy cars
plastic bread ties
marbles
cotton balls
bottle caps
poker chips
paper clips
clothespins
erasers

Multimedia:

The following resources can be found in educational catalogs:

1. *Number Fun* [record]. Melody House Records.

2. "The Number Rock," *We All Live Together Series—Vol. 2* [record]. Youngheart Records.

3. "1, 2, Buckle My Shoe," *We All Live Together Series—Vol. 3* [record]. Youngheart Records.

4. *Numbers* [record]. Sesame Street Records.

5. *Early Math* [IBM/Mac/Windows software, PK–2]. Bright Star.

6. *Mathosaurus* [IBM software PK–K and K–2]. Micrograms.

7. *Numbers…What They Mean* [30-minute video]. Edu-vid.

8. *Learning Your Numbers* [30-minute video]. Edu-vid.

9. *Hello Number* [30-minute video]. Edu-vid.

10. *Ten Little Robots* [Apple/IBM software, PK and lower]. Unicorn.

11. *Math and Me* [Apple/IBM software, PK–2]. Davidson.

12. *Stickybear Numbers* [Apple/IBM software, PK–1]. Optimum Resources.

Books:

The following books can be used to complement the theme:

1. Hutchins, Pat. (1986). *The Doorbell Rang*. New York: Scholastic.

2. Aker, Suzanne. (1990). *What Comes in Twos, Threes, & Fours?* New York: Simon & Schuster.

3. Anno, Mitsumasa. (1992). *Anno's Counting Book Big Book.* New York: Harper Collins.

4. Carle, Eric. (1985). *My Very First Book of Numbers.* New York: Harper Collins.

5. Gillen, Patricia B. (1987). *My Signing Book of Numbers.* Washington, DC: Gallaudet University Press.

6. Holmes, Stephen. (1990). *Hidden Numbers.* San Diego: Harcourt Brace Jovanovich.

7. Oliver, Stephen. (1990). *My First Look at Numbers.* New York: Random House.

8. Pomerantz, Charlotte. (1987). *How Many Trucks Can a Tow Truck Tow?* New York: Random House.

9. Bang, Molly. (1986). *Ten, Nine, Eight.* New York: Greenwillow.

10. Giganti, Paul, Jr. (1988). *How Many Snails?* New York: Greenwillow.

11. Hort, Lenny. (1991). *How Many Stars in the Sky?* New York: Tambourine.

12. Grossman, Virginia, & Long, Sylvia. (1991). *Ten Little Rabbits.* San Francisco: Chronicle Books.

13. Bryant-Mole, K. (1992). *Numbers.* Tulsa, OK: EDC Publishing.

14. *Moja Means One: A Swahili Counting Book.* (1987). New York: Dial Books for Young Readers.

15. Lottridge, Celia B. (1900). *One Watermelon Seed.* New York: Oxford University Press, Inc.

16. Moss, David. (1989). *Numbers.* Avenal, NJ: Outlet Book Inc.

17. Tucker, Sian. (1992). *Numbers.* New York: Simon and Schuster Trade.

18. Tudor, Tasha. (1988). *One Is One.* New York: Macmillan Children's Book Group.

19. Walsh, Abigail. (1992). *Exploring the Numbers One to Ten.* Mankato, MN: Capstone Press, Inc.

20. Zimmerman, H. Werner. (1990). *Alphonse Knows...Zero Is Not Enough.* New York: Oxford University Press.

THEME 16

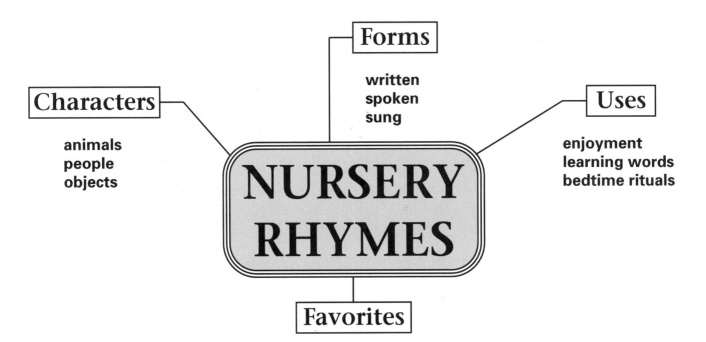

Forms

written
spoken
sung

Characters

animals
people
objects

Uses

enjoyment
learning words
bedtime rituals

NURSERY RHYMES

Favorites

Little Bo Peep
Mary Had a Little Lamb
Old Mother Hubbard
Hey Diddle Diddle
Little Miss Muffet
Humpty Dumpty
Jack and Jill
Mary Mary Quite Contrary

Jack Be Nimble
Rub-A-Dub-Dub
The Muffin Man
Little Jack Horner
Old MacDonald Had A Farm
Two Little Blackbirds
Hickory Dickory Dock
Three Kittens' Mittens

Theme Goals:

Through participating in the experiences provided by this theme, the children may learn:

1. Favorite nursery rhymes.

2. Uses of nursery rhymes.

3. Forms of nursery rhymes.

4. Characters portrayed in nursery rhymes.

Concepts for the Children to Learn:

1. Nursery rhymes are fun to listen to and say.

2. Nursery rhymes can contain real or pretend words.

3. Some nursery rhymes are about animals.

4. Some nursery rhymes help us learn numbers and counting.

5. Some nursery rhymes teach us about different people.

Vocabulary:

nursery rhyme—short, simple poem or rhyme.

Bulletin Board

The purpose of this bulletin board is to promote name recognition and call attention to the printed word. This is a check-in bulletin board. Each child is provided a bulletin board piece with his name printed on it. When the children arrive each morning at school, they hang their name on the bulletin board. To create a "Find Your Mitten" bulletin board, cut a mitten out of tagboard for each child in the class. Three kittens can be constructed and attached to the bulletin board to represent the three little kittens who lost their mittens. Use a paper punch to cut a hole in the top of each mitten. Hang push pins on the bulletin board for the children to hang their mittens on during the course of the day.

Parent Letter

Dear Parents,

Nursery rhymes will be the focus of our next theme. These rhymes can serve as a bridge between the home and school. I'm sure many of you have shared favorite nursery rhymes with your child at home. Nursery rhymes are an easy introduction to poetry, as well as the concept of rhyming words.

At School

We have a fun-filled curriculum planned for our unit on nursery rhymes. A few highlights include:

- acting out various rhymes with puppets that represent different characters from familiar nursery rhymes.
- unraveling the riddle of the "Humpty Dumpty" nursery rhyme. (Why couldn't Humpty be put back together? Because Humpty was an egg!)
- creating "Little Miss Muffet" spiders in the art area.
- taking turns being nimble and quick as we jump over a candlestick to dramatize the rhyme of "Jack Be Nimble."

At Home

To foster concepts of the unit at home, try the following:

- Let your child help you crack eggs open to make scrambled eggs. Children like to feel that they have accomplished a grown-up task when they crack the eggs.
- Sing or recite some of the many rhymes your child already knows such as, "Jack and Jill," and, "Mary Had a Little Lamb." These also develop an enjoyment of music and singing.

Share a nursery rhyme with your child today!

Reciting nursery rhymes can help relax a child.

Music:

1. **"Hickory Dickory Dock"** (traditional)

   Hickory dickory dock
   The mouse ran up the clock.
   The clock struck one, the mouse ran down,
   Hickory dickory dock.

2. **"The Muffin Man"** (traditional)

   Oh, do you know the muffin man,
   The muffin man, the muffin man?
   Oh, do you know the muffin man
   Who lives on Dreary Lane?

   Yes, I know the muffin man…

3. **"Two Little Blackbirds"** (traditional)

   Two little blackbirds sitting on a hill
   One named Jack. One named Jill.

Fly away, Jack. Fly away, Jill.
Come back, Jack. Come back, Jill.
Two little blackbirds sitting on a hill.
One named Jack. One named Jill.

4. **"Jack and Jill"** (traditional)

   Jack and Jill went up a hill
   To fetch a pail of water.
   Jack fell down and broke his crown
   And Jill fell tumbling after.

Fingerplays:

LITTLE JACK HORNER

   Little Jack Horner
   Sat in a corner
   Eating a Christmas pie.
      (pretend you're eating)
   He put in his thumb,
      (thumb down)
   And pulled out a plum
      (thumb up)
   And said, "What a good boy am I!"
      (say out loud)

PAT-A-CAKE

   Pat-a-cake, pat-a-cake, baker's man.
   Bake me a cake as fast as you can!
      (clap hands together lightly)
   Roll it
      (roll hands)
   And pat it
      (touch hands together lightly)
   And mark it with a "B"
      (write "b" in the air)
   And put it in the oven for baby and me.
      (point to baby and to yourself)

WEE WILLIE WINKLE

   Wee Willie Winkle runs through the town
      (pretend to run)
   Upstairs, downstairs in his nightgown,
      (point up, point down, then point to clothes)
   Rapping at the window, crying through the lock
      (knock in the air, peek through a hole)
   "Are the children all in bed, for now it's eight o'clock?"
      (shake finger)

OLD KING COLE

Old King Cole was a merry old soul
   (lift elbows up and down)
And a merry old soul was he.
   (nod head)
He called for his pipe.
   (clap two times)
He called for his bowl.
   (clap two times)
And he called for his fiddlers three.
   (clap two times then pretend to play violin)

HICKORY DICKORY DOCK

Hickory dickory dock
   (swing arms back and forth together, bent
   down low)
The mouse ran up the clock.
   (run fingers up your arm)
The clock struck one
   (clap, and then hold up one finger)
The mouse ran down.
   (run fingers down your arm)
Hickory dickory dock.
   (swing arms back and forth together, bent
   down low)

Science:

1. **Mary's Garden**

   A styrofoam cup with the child's name printed
   on it and a scoop of soil should be provided.
   Then let everyone choose a flower seed. Be
   sure to save the seed packages. The children
   can plant their seed, water, and care for it.
   When the plant begins to grow, try to identify
   the names of the plants by comparing them to
   pictures on the seed packages.

2. **Hickory Dickory Dock Clock**

   Draw and cut a large Hickory Dickory Dock
   clock from cardboard. Move the hands of the
   clock and see if the children can identify the
   numeral.

3. **Wool**

   Pieces of wool fabric mounted on cardboard
   can be matched with samples.

4. **Pumpkin Tasters**

   Plan a Peter, Peter, Pumpkin Eater pumpkin-
   tasting party.

Dramatic Play:

1. **Baker**

   Baking props such as hats, aprons, cookie
   cutters, baking pans, rolling pins, mixers,
   spoons, and bowls can be placed in the
   dramatic play area.

2. **Puppets**

   A puppet theater can be placed in the dramatic
   play area for the duration of the unit. To add
   variety, each day a different set of puppets can
   be added for the children.

Arts and Crafts:

1. **Spiders**

   Add black tempera paint to a playdough
   mixture. In addition to the playdough, provide
   black pipe cleaners or yarn. Using these
   materials, spiders or other objects can be
   created.

2. **Spider Webs**

   Cut circles of black paper to fit in the bottom of
   a pie tin. Mix thin silver or white tempera
   paint. Place a marble and two teaspoons of
   paint on the paper. Gently tilt the pie tin,
   allowing the marble to roll through the paint,
   creating a spider web design.

3. **Twinkle Twinkle Little Stars**

   The children can decorate stars with glitter and
   sequins. The stars can be hung from the ceiling
   and during group time sing "Twinkle,
   Twinkle, Little Star."

4. **Little Boy Blue's Horn**

   Collect paper towel tubes. The tubes can be
   painted with tempera. When the tubes are dry,

cover one end with tissue paper and secure with a rubber band. The children can use them as horns.

Sensory:

Water and Pails

Add water, pails, and scoopers to the sensory table.

Large Muscle:

1. **Jack Be Nimble's Candlestick**

   Make a candlestick out of an old paper towel holder and tissue paper for the flame. Repeat the rhyme by substituting each child's name.

   Jack be nimble. Jack be quick.
   Jack jump over the candlestick.

2. **Wall Building**

   Encourage the children to create a large wall out of blocks for Humpty Dumpty. Act out the rhyme.

Field Trips/Resource People:

1. **Candlemaking**

   Invite a resource person to demonstrate candlemaking, or take a field trip to a craft center so that the children can view candles being made.

2. **Greenhouse**

   Visit a florist or greenhouse to observe flowers and plants.

Math:

1. **Puzzles**

   Draw or cut out several pictures of different nursery rhymes ("Jack and Jill," "Jack Be

Nimble," etc.) and mount on tagboard. Laminate and cut each picture into five to seven pieces. The children can match nursery rhyme puzzle pieces.

2. **Rote Counting**

   Say or sing the following nursery rhyme to help the children with rote counting:

   1, 2 buckle my shoe
   3, 4 shut the door
   5, 6 pick up sticks
   7, 8 lay them straight
   9, 10 a big fat hen.

3. **Matching**

   Draw from one to 10 simple figures from a nursery rhyme (mittens, candlesticks, pails, etc.) on the left side of a sheet of tagboard and the corresponding numeral on the right side. Laminate the pieces and cut each in half creating different-shaped puzzle pieces. The children can match the number of figures to the corresponding numeral.

4. **Mitten Match**

   Collect several matching pairs of mittens. Mix them up and have children match the pairs.

Social Studies:

Table Setting

On a sheet of tagboard, trace the outline of a plate, cup, knife, fork, spoon, and napkin. Laminate. The children can match the silverware and dishes to the outline on the placemat in preparation for snack or meals. This activity can be extended by having the children turn the placemat over, and arrange the place setting without the aid of an outline.

Group Time (games, language):

Old Mother Hubbard's Doggie Bone Game

Save a bone or construct one from tagboard. Ask one child to volunteer to be the doggie.

146

Seat the children in a circle with the doggie in the center and the bone in front of him. The doggie closes his eyes. A child from the circle quietly comes and steals the bone. When the child is reseated with the bone out of sight, the children will call,

"Doggie, doggie, where's your bone?
Someone took it from your home!"

The doggie gets three chances to guess who has the bone. If he guesses correctly, the child who took the bone becomes the doggie.

Cooking:

1. **Bran Muffins**

   (Use with the "Muffin Man" rhyme)

   3 cups whole wheat bran cereal
   1 cup boiling water
   1/2 cup shortening or oil
   2 eggs
   2 1/2 cups unbleached flour
   1 1/2 cups sugar
   2 1/2 teaspoons baking soda
   2 cups buttermilk

   Preheat the oven to 400 degrees. Line the muffin tins with paper baking cups. In a large bowl combine the cereal and boiling water. Stir in the shortening and eggs. Add the remaining ingredients. Blend well. Spoon the batter into cups about 3/4 full. Bake at 400 degrees for 18 to 22 minutes or until golden brown. Eat at snack time and sing the "Muffin Man" song.

2. **Humpty Dumpty Pear Salad**

   For each serving provide 1/2 pear, 1 lifesaver, 1 tablespoon mayonnaise, 2 cherries, 1 raisin, and a lettuce leaf. The children can prepare their own salad. To do this each child puts a lettuce leaf on a plate and places a pear half on top of it, round side up. Then add the two cherries for eyes, a raisin for a nose, and the piece of lifesaver candy for a mouth. Add mayonnaise to taste.

   Source: Graham, Terry. (1982). *Let Loose on Mother Goose*. Terry Graham. Incentive Publishing Company.

3. **Cottage Cheese***

   2 quarts pasteurized skim milk (to make approximately 3/4 pounds of cottage cheese)
   salt
   liquid rennet or a junket tablet

   Heat the water to 80 degrees Fahrenheit in the bottom part of a double boiler. Use a thermometer to determine the water temperature. Do not guess.

   Pour the skim milk into the top of the double boiler. Dilute 1 or 2 drops of liquid rennet in a tablespoon of cold water and stir it into the milk. If rennet is not available, add 1/8 of a junket tablet to a tablespoon of water and add it to the milk. Allow the milk to remain at 80 degrees until it curdles, in about 12 to 18 hours. During this period no special attention is necessary. If desired, the milk may be placed in a warm oven overnight. Place the curd in a cheese cloth over a container to drain the whey. Occasionally, pour out the whey that collects in the container so that the draining will continue. In 15 to 20 minutes, the curd will become mushy and will drain more slowly. When it is almost firm and the whey has nearly ceased to flow, the cheese is ready for salting and eating. Salt the cheese to taste. The cottage cheese can be spread on crackers for a snack.

   * This activity is time-consuming; consequently, it may be more appropriate for older children.

4. **Miss Muffet's Curds and Whey**

   2 cups whole milk
   1 teaspoon vinegar

   Warm milk and add vinegar. Stir as curds separate from the whey. Curds are the milk solids and the whey is the liquid that is poured off. You can let your children taste the whey but they probably will not be thrilled by it. Strain the curds from the whey, then dump the curds onto a paper towel and gently press the curds with more towels to get out the liquid. Sprinkle with salt and refrigerate. Eat as cottage cheese. You can also serve the curds at room temperature. Stir them until they are smooth. Add different flavorings (such as cinnamon, orange flavoring, vanilla, etc.). Use as a spread on crackers. Curds mixed with peanut butter is great. Serves 12 (2 crackers each).

Multimedia:

The following resources can be found in educational catalogs:

1. *More Mother Goose with the Play-Along at Home Rhythm Band* [record]. (1962). A Disney Land Record, Walt Disney Production.

2. Jenkins, Ella. *Nursery Rhymes—Rhyming and Remembering* [record].

3. *Mother Goose* [record]. Melody House.

Books:

The following books can be used to complement the theme:

1. Aylesworth, Jim. (1992). *The Cat & the Fiddle & More*. New York: Macmillan.

2. Baker, Keith. (1994). *Big Fat Hen*. San Diego: Harcourt Brace Jovanovich.

3. Beck, Ian. (1993). *Five Little Ducks*. New York: Henry Hold & Co.

4. Craig, Helen. (1993). *I See the Moon & the Moon Sees Me*. New York: Harper Collins.

5. Demi. (1986). *Dragon Kites & Dragonflies: A Collection of Chinese Nursery Rhymes*. San Diego: Harcourt Brace Jovanovich.

6. Langley, Jonathan. (1991). *Rain, Rain, Go Away! A Book of Nursery Rhymes*. New York: Dial.

7. Lewis, J. Patrick. (1991). *Two Legged, Four-Legged, No Legged Rhymes*. New York: Alfred A. Knopf.

8. Officer, Robyn. (1992). *Mother Goose's Nursery Rhymes*. Kansas City: Andrews & McMeel.

9. Wyndham, Robert. (1989). *Chinese Mother Goose*. New York: Putnam.

10. Young, Ed. (1989). *Lon Po Po: A Red Riding Hood Story from China*. New York: Putnam.

11. Hale, Sarah J. (1990). *Mary Had a Little Lamb*. New York: Scholastic Inc.

12. Hennessy, B. G. (1991). *The Missing Tarts*. New York: Puffin Books.

13. Hopkins, Lee B. (1989). *Animals from Mother Goose*. San Diego: Harcourt Brace Jovanovich.

14. Hopkins, Lee B. (1989). *People from Mother Goose*. San Diego: Harcourt Brace Jovanovich.

15. Kemp, Moira (Illus.). (1991). *Baa, Baa, Black Sheep*. New York: Dutton Children's Books.

16. Kemp, Moira (Illus.). (1991). *Hey Diddle Diddle*. New York: Dutton Children's Books.

17. Kemp, Moira (Illus.). (1991). *Hickory Dickory Dock*. New York: Dutton Children's Books.

18. Kemp, Moira (Illus.). (1991). *This Little Piggy*. New York: Dutton Children's Books.

19. Langley, Jonathan. (1991). *Rain, Rain, Go Away! A Book of Nursery Rhymes*. New York: Dial Books for Young Readers.

20. McGee, Shelagh. (1992). *I'm a Little Teapot*. New York: Doubleday and Co.

21. Marshall, James. (1991). *Old Mother Hubbard and Her Wonderful Dog*. New York: Farrar, Straus and Giroux, Inc.

22. Wildsmith, Brian. (1987). *Mother Goose: Nursery Rhymes*. New York: Oxford University Press, Inc.

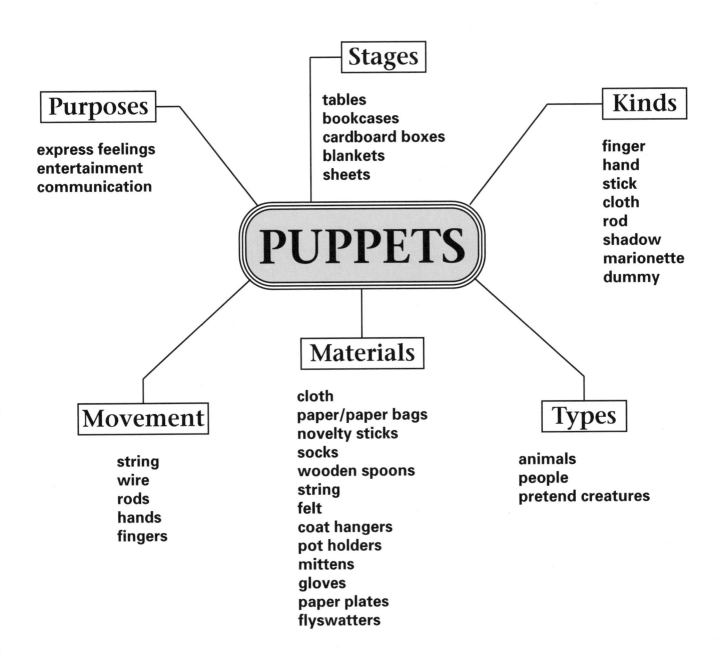

Stages

tables
bookcases
cardboard boxes
blankets
sheets

Purposes

express feelings
entertainment
communication

Kinds

finger
hand
stick
cloth
rod
shadow
marionette
dummy

PUPPETS

Materials

cloth
paper/paper bags
novelty sticks
socks
wooden spoons
string
felt
coat hangers
pot holders
mittens
gloves
paper plates
flyswatters

Movement

string
wire
rods
hands
fingers

Types

animals
people
pretend creatures

Theme Goals:

Through participating in the experiences provided by this theme, the children may learn:

1. The purpose of using puppets.

2. Kinds of puppets.

3. Types of puppets.

4. Materials used to make puppets.

5. Ways of moving puppets.

6. Types of puppet stages.

Concepts for the Children to Learn:

1. Puppets can be fun.

2. Puppets can be used for communicating and entertainment.

3. We can use puppets to express feelings.

4. People talk for puppets.

5. Puppets can be made from paper, cloth, or even wood.

6. Puppets can be made to look like animals, people, or pretend creatures.

7. Puppets can be moved with hands or fingers.

8. Mittens, gloves, and paper plates can all be made into puppets.

9. Large boxes can be used for puppet stages.

Vocabulary:

1. **puppet**—a toy that is moved by the hand or finger.

2. **marionette**—a puppet with strings for movement.

3. **puppet show**—a story told with puppets.

4. **puppeteer**—a person who makes a puppet move and speak.

5. **puppet stage**—a place for puppets to act.

6. **entertainment**—things we enjoy seeing and listening to.

7. **imaginary**—something that is not real.

Bulletin Board

The purpose of this bulletin board is to show a variety of puppets. The children's expressive language skills will be stimulated by interacting with the puppets. Design the bulletin board by constructing about five or six simple puppets for the children to take off the bulletin board to play with. Include a flyswatter puppet, a paper bag puppet, hand puppet, sock puppet, and a wooden spoon puppet. Hooks or push pins can be used to attach the puppets to the bulletin board.

Parent Letter

Dear Parents,

Our new unit will focus on puppets. They are magical and motivating to young children. Sometimes a child will respond or talk to a puppet in a situation when he might not talk to an adult or other child. Through learning experiences involving puppets, the children will become aware of the different types of puppets and materials that can be used to make puppets. They will express themselves creatively and imaginatively.

At School

Some of the activities related to puppets include:

- creating our own puppets with a variety of materials.
- using the puppet stage throughout the week, putting on puppet shows for one and all.
- exploring various types of puppets, including finger, hand, stick, shadow, and marionette puppets.

At Home

The children enjoy retelling familiar stories and making up original stories for puppet characters. To stimulate this type of play, you and your child can make simple puppets at home with objects found around the house.

Paper Bag Puppets—Using small paper lunch bags, children can use crayons or markers to create a puppet. The fold in the bag can be used as the mouth. After the child's hand is in the bag, the puppet can talk. Yarn scraps can easily be glued on for hair and construction paper scraps can add a decorative touch.
Sock Puppets—I'm sure you have a couple of socks around the house that seem to have lost their mates. (Does your dryer eat socks, too?) Depending on your child's skills and how much supervision you can provide—eyes, a nose, and hair of a variety of materials (yarn, buttons, fabric) can either be sewn or glued on. Insert your hand and your puppet is ready!
Stick Puppets—Make story characters' faces or bodies on heavy paper or on cardboard with crayons, markers, or paint. Cut the figures out and attach them with strong glue or tape to a ruler, popsicle stick, tongue depressor, or any stick that can be used to hold the puppet and move it. A large box or table can serve as the puppet stage.

Enjoy your child!

Young children become engrossed in puppet shows.

Music:

"Eensy Weensy Spider" (traditional)

Fingerplays:

CATERPILLAR CRAWLING

One little caterpillar crawled on my shoe.
Another came along and then there were two.
Two little caterpillars crawled on my knee.
Another came along and then there were three.
Three little caterpillars crawled on the floor.
Another came along and then there were four.
Four little caterpillars watch them crawl away.
They'll all turn into butterflies some fine day.

This fingerplay can be told using puppets
made from felt or tagboard.

Source: Indenbaum, Valerie, & Shapior,
Marcia. (1983). *The Everything Book*. Chicago:
Partner Press.

SPECKLED FROGS

Five green-speckled frogs
Sitting on a speckled log

Eating the most delicious bugs,
Yum, yum!
　(rub tummy)

One jumped into the pool
Where it was nice and cool
Now there are four green-speckled frogs.

Repeat until there are no green-speckled frogs.

This fingerplay can be told using puppets
made from felt or tagboard.

CHICKADEES

Five little chickadees sitting in a door
　(hold up hand)
One flew away and then there were four
　(put down one finger at a time)
Four little chickadees sitting in a tree
One flew away and then there were three.
Three little chickadees looking at you.
One flew away and then there were two.
Two little chickadees sitting in the sun.
One flew away and then there was one.
One little chickadee sitting all alone.
He flew away and then there were none.

This fingerplay can be told using puppets
made from felt or tagboard.

Science:

1. Classify Puppets

During group time let the children classify the various puppets into special categories such as animals, people, insects, imaginary things, etc.

2. Button Box

A large box of buttons should be provided. The children can sort the buttons according to color, size, or shape into a muffin tin or egg carton.

Dramatic Play:

1. Puppet Show

A puppet stage should be available throughout the entire unit in the dramatic play area. Change or add the puppets on a regular basis using as many different kinds of puppets as possible.

2. Puppet Shop

A variety of materials should be provided for the children to construct puppets. Include items such as buttons, bows, felt, paper bags, cloth pieces, socks, tongue depressors, etc.

Arts and Crafts:

1. Making Puppets

Puppets can be made from almost any material. Some suggestions are listed here:

- cotton covered with cloth attached to a tongue depressor.
- paper sacks stuffed with newspaper.
- a cork for a head with a hole in it for a finger.
- socks.
- cardboard colored with crayon attached to a tongue depressor.
- flyswatter.
- oatmeal box attached to a dowel.
- nylon panty hose stretched over a hanger bent into an oval shape.
- empty toilet paper and paper towel rolls.

2. Puppet Stages

Puppet stages can be made from the following materials:

- boxes, including tempera paint and markers for decorating.
- large paper bags.
- half-gallon milk carton.
- towel draped over an arm.
- towel draped over the back of a chair.
- blanket covering a card table.

Sensory:

Sensory Table

During this unit add to the sensory table all of the various materials that puppets are made of:

- string
- buttons
- felt
- toilet paper rolls
- cardboard
- paper
- sticks
- wood shavings

Large Muscle:

1. Creative Movement

Demonstrate how to manipulate a marionette. Then have the children pretend that they are marionettes and that they have strings attached to their arms and legs. Say, "Someone is pulling up the string that is attached to your arm, what would happen to your arm?" Allow the children to make that movement. Continue with other movements.

2. Large Puppets

Large puppets such as stick or rod puppets can provide the children with a lot of large muscle movement.

3. **Pin the Nose on the Puppet**

This game is a variation of the traditional "Pin the Tail on the Donkey." (This game would be more appropriate for five-, six-, seven-, and eight-year-old children.)

Field Trips/Resource People:

1. **Puppet Show**

Place puppets by the puppet stage to encourage the children to put on puppet shows.

2. **Puppeteer**

Invite a puppeteer to visit the classroom and show the children the many uses of puppets.

Math:

1. **Examine a Puppet**

With the children, examine a puppet and count all of its various parts. Count its eyes, legs, arms, stripes on its shirt, etc. Discuss how it was constructed.

2. **Puppet Dot-to-Dot**

Draw a large puppet on a sheet of tagboard. Laminate or cover the tagboard sheet with clear adhesive paper. A grease pencil or felt-tip watercolor marker should be provided for the children to draw. Also, felt scraps should be available to remove grease markings. Otherwise, a damp cloth or paper towel should be available.

Social Studies:

Occupation Puppets

Introduce various types of occupation puppets. Ask the children to describe each.

Group Time (games, language):

Puppet Show

Using your favorite classroom stories, put on a puppet show. The children can volunteer to be the various characters. Pre-tape the story so that the children can listen to it while they practice. This might be a good activity to invite parents to attend.

Cooking:

1. **Puppet Faces**

Make open-faced sandwiches using peanut butter or cream cheese spread onto a slice of bread or a bun. Carrot curls can be used to represent hair. Raisins and green or purple grape halves can be used for the eyes, nose, and mouth.

2. **Dog Puppet Salad**

Place a pear half onto the plate. Two apple slices can be added to resemble a dog's ears hanging down. Then raisins or grape halves can be used to represent the eyes and nose of a dog.

Multimedia:

The following resource can be found in educational catalogs:

"The Little Red Hen Operetta," *Puppet Parade* [record]. Melody House Records.

Books:

The following books can be used to complement the theme:

1. Hoyt-Goldsmith, Diane. (1991). *Pueblo Storyteller.* New York: Holiday.

2. Poskanzer, Susan C. (1989). *Puppeteer.* Mahwah, NJ: Troll Associates.

3. Bridwell, Norman. (1991). *Hello Clifford: A Puppet Book.* New York: Scholastic Inc.

4. Chaney, Steve. (1989). *The Puppet in the Big Black Box.* Sunnyvale, CA: Stiff Lip Productions.

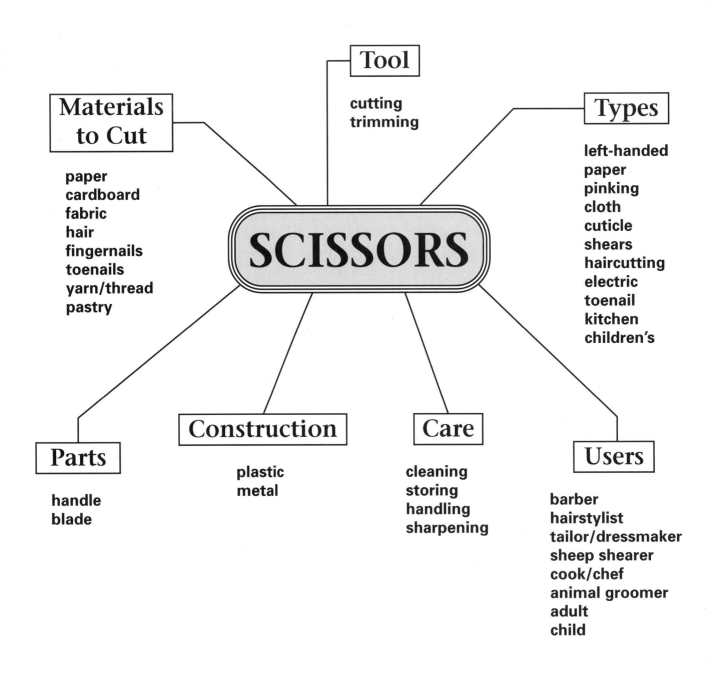

Tool
cutting
trimming

**Materials
to Cut**
paper
cardboard
fabric
hair
fingernails
toenails
yarn/thread
pastry

Types
left-handed
paper
pinking
cloth
cuticle
shears
haircutting
electric
toenail
kitchen
children's

SCISSORS

Parts
handle
blade

Construction
plastic
metal

Care
cleaning
storing
handling
sharpening

Users
barber
hairstylist
tailor/dressmaker
sheep shearer
cook/chef
animal groomer
adult
child

Theme Goals:

Through participating in the experiences provided by this theme, the children may learn:

1. Parts of scissors.

2. Uses of scissors.

3. Materials that can be cut with scissors.

4. Care of scissors.

5. People who use scissors.

6. Sizes and shapes of scissors.

Concepts for the Children to Learn:

1. Scissors are tools.

2. Scissors help us do our work.

3. Scissors cut paper, fingernails, hair, and material.

4. There are many types of scissors.

5. Some people need scissors for their job.

6. Hand motions make scissors cut.

7. Scissors need to be handled carefully.

Vocabulary:

1. **blade**—cutting edge of scissors.

2. **pinking shears**—sewing scissors.

3. **shears**—large scissors.

Bulletin Board

The purpose of this bulletin board is to have the children match the colored scissors to the corresponding colored skein. To prepare the bulletin board, construct six scissors out of tagboard. With felt-tip markers, color each one a different color and laminate. Fasten the scissors to the top of the bulletin board. Next, construct six skeins of yarn out of tagboard. Color each skein a different color to correspond with the scissors. Attach the skeins to the bottom part of the bulletin board. Fasten a string to each of the scissors and a push pin to each of the skeins of yarn.

Parent Letter

Dear Parents,

Snip, snip, snip! This sound will be heard frequently in the classroom as we start a unit on scissors. Through the experiences provided, the children will be introduced to various kinds and uses of scissors. They will also learn the proper care and safety precautions to consider when handling and using scissors.

At School

Some activities related to scissors will include:

- discussing safety and proper uses of scissors.
- experimenting cutting with different kinds of scissors.
- cutting a variety of materials such as yarn, fabric, paper, wallpaper, and aluminum foil.
- visiting Tom's Barber Shop on Wednesday morning. We will be leaving at 10:00 A.M. and expect to watch a haircut demonstration. Also, we will observe the tools and equipment used by a barber.

At Home

Children need many experiences working with scissors before they are able to master cutting skills. Each child will learn this skill at his own rate. To assist your child, save scraps of paper and allow your child to practice cutting them using child-sized scissors. Once the cutting skills have been mastered, your child may enjoy cutting coupons out of newspaper sections or magazines.

Have fun with your child!

Some children need left-handed scissors; others can use right-handed scissors.

Fingerplay:

OPEN SHUT THEM

Open, shut them, open, shut them.
  (use index and middle finger to make scissors motion)
Give a little snip, snip, snip.
  (three quick snips with fingers)
Open, shut them, open, shut them.
  (repeat scissors motion)
Make another clip.
  (make another scissor motion)

Science:

1. **Scissor Show**

    Place a variety of scissors on an overhead projector. Encourage the children to describe each by naming it and explaining its use.

2. **Shadow Profiles**

    Tape a piece of paper on a wall or bulletin board. Stand a child in front of the paper. Shine a light source to create a shadow of the head. Trace each child's shadow. Provide scissors for the children to cut out their own shadows.

3. **Weighing Scissors**

    On the science table, place a variety of scissors and a scale. The children should be encouraged to note the differences in weight.

Dramatic Play:

1. **Beauty Shop**

    Set up a beauty shop in the dramatic play area. Include items such as curling irons, hair dryers, combs, and wigs. Also, include a chair, plastic covering, and Beauty Shop sign. A cash register and money can be added to encourage play. (For safety purposes, cut the cords off the hair dryer and curling irons.)

2. **Tailor/Dressmaking Shop**

    Materials that are easy to cut should be provided. Likewise, a variety of scissors should be placed next to the material. Older children may want to make doll clothes.

3. **Bake Shop**

    Playdough, scissors, and other cooking tools can be placed on a table. If desired, make paper baker hats and a sign.

4. **Dog Groomer**

    A dog grooming area can be set up in the dramatic play corner with stuffed animals, brushes, and combs. If available, cut off the cord of an electric dog shaver and provide for the children.

Arts and Crafts:

1. **Scissor Snip**

    Strips of paper with scissors can be provided for snipping.

2. Cutting

For experimentation, a wide variety of materials and types of scissors can be added to the art area for the children.

Sensory:

Playdough

Scissors can be placed next to the playdough in the sensory area.

Field Trips/Resource People:

1. Hairstylist

Visit a hairstylist. While there, observe a person's hair being cut. Notice the different scissors that are used and how they are used.

2. Pet Groomer

Invite a pet groomer to class. If possible, arrange for a dog to be groomed.

Math:

Shape Sort

Cut out different-colored shapes. Place the shapes on a table for the children to sort by color, shape, and size.

Group Time (games, language):

Scissor Safety

Discuss safety while using scissors. The children can help make a list of "How we use our scissors safely." Display chart in room.

Cooking:

Pretzels

1 1/2 cups warm water
1 envelope yeast
4 cups flour
1 teaspoon salt
1 tablespoon sugar
coarse salt
egg

Mix the warm water, yeast, and sugar together. Set this mixture aside for 5 minutes. Pour salt and flour into a bowl. Add the yeast mixture to make dough. Roll the dough into a long snake form. Cut the dough into smaller sections using scissors. The children can then form individual shapes with dough. Brush egg on the shapes with pastry brush and sprinkle with salt. Preheat the oven and bake pretzels at 425 degrees for 12 minutes.

PASTES

Bookmaker's Paste

1 teaspoon flour
2 teaspoons cornstarch
1/4 teaspoon powdered alum
3 ounces water

Mix dry ingredients. Add water slowly, stirring out all lumps. Cook over slow fire (preferably in a double boiler), stirring constantly. Remove when paste begins to thicken. It will thicken more as it cools. Keep in covered jars. Thin with water if necessary.

Cooked Flour Paste

1 cup boiling water

1 tablespoon powdered alum
1 pint cold water
1 pint flour
1 heaping teaspoon oil of cloves
oil of wintergreen (optional)

To 1 cup boiling water add powdered alum. Mix flour and fold in water until smooth; pour

---

mixture gradually into boiling alum water. Cook until it has a bluish cast, stirring all the time. Remove from fire, add oil of cloves, and stir well. Keep in airtight jars. Thin when necessary by adding water. A drop or two of oil of wintergreen may be added to give the paste a pleasing aroma.

Colored Salt Paste

Mix 2 parts salt to 1 part flour. Add powdered paint and enough water to make a smooth heavy paste. Keep in airtight container.

Crepe Paper Paste

Cut or tear 2 tablespoons crepe paper of a single color. The finer the paper is cut, the smoother the paste will be. Add 1/2 tablespoon flour, 1/2 tablespoon salt, and enough water to make a paste. Stir and squash the mixture until it is as smooth as possible. Store in airtight container.

Books:

The following books can be used to complement the theme:

1. Girard, Linda Walvoord. (1986). *Jeremy's First Haircut*. Niles, IL: Albert Whitman and Co.

2. Lillegard, Dee. (1987). *I Can Be a Beautician*. Chicago: Children's Press.

3. Brown, Laurene, & Brown, Marc. (1986). *Visiting the Art Museum*. New York: Dutton.

4. dePaola, Tomie. (1989). *Haircuts for the Woolseys*. New York: Putnam.

5. Reiss, John J. (1987). *Shapes*. New York: Macmillan.

6. Frandsen, Karen G. (1986). *Michael's New Haircut*. Chicago, IL: Children's Press.

7. Tusa, Tricia. (1991). *Camilla's New Hairdo*. New York: Farrar, Straus and Giroux.

Names

circle
triangle
rectangle
square
oval

Construction

lines
round
four sides
three sides

SHAPES

Theme Goals:

Through participating in the experiences provided by this theme, the children may learn:

1. The names of basic shapes.

2. Identification of basic shapes.

3. Objects have shapes.

Concepts for the Children to Learn:

1. There are many shapes of different sizes and colors in our world.

2. Some shapes have names.

3. A circle is round.

4. Triangles have three sides.

5. Rectangles and squares have four sides.

6. All objects contain one or more shapes.

7. We can draw lines to make shapes.

Vocabulary:

1. **circle**—a shape that is round.

2. **rectangle**—a shape with four sides.

3. **square**—a shape with four sides of equal length.

4. **triangle**—a shape with three sides.

5. **line**—a mark made with a pencil, crayon, etc., to make a shape.

6. **oval**—shaped like an egg.

Bulletin Board

The purpose of this bulletin board is to have the child make a shape train. To prepare the bulletin board use the model shown to construct a train using basic shapes. Color the shapes and laminate. Trace laminated shapes onto black construction paper to construct shadow shapes. Staple shadow shapes onto board in train pattern. By using magnets, the children can affix the colored shape pieces to the shadows.

Parent Letter

Dear Parents,

Hello again! Shapes will be the focus of our new unit. Our world consists of shapes. The children will become aware of this on an introductory walk around the block. They will become familiar with the names of shapes and will also classify objects according to shape. Consequently, the children will be more aware of all the shapes in our world. In addition, the children who are developmentally ready will practice drawing some of the basic shapes.

At School

Some of the fun-filled learning activities scheduled for this unit include:

- playing a game called "Shape Basket Upset."
- listening to the story, *Shapes and Things*, by Tana Hoban.
- feeling and identifying objects by shape in a feely box.
- making and baking cookies of various shapes.

At Home

You can reinforce the activities included in this unit at home by observing shaped objects in your house. Each day at school we will have a special shape theme. Your child can bring in an object from home to fit the shape of the day. I will send home the shape the night before so you and your child will have time to look for an object. The following fingerplay can be recited to foster language and memory skills.

Circle and Square

Close my eyes, shut them tight.
(close eyes)
Make a circle with my one hand.
(make a circle with one hand)
Keep them shut; make it fair.
(keep eyes shut)
With my other hand, make a square.
(make a square with other hand)

Enjoy your child!

What can you make with these shapes?

Music:

The following songs can be found in Butler, Talmadge, Kirkland, Terry, & Leach. (1975). *Music for Today's Young Children*. Broadman Press.

1. "Colors, Shapes, and Numbers"

2. "Different Shapes"

Fingerplays:

RIGHT CIRCLE, LEFT SQUARE

Close my eyes, shut them tight.
   (close eyes)
Make a circle with my one hand.
   (make circle with one hand)
Keep them shut; make it fair.
   (keep eyes shut)
With my other hand, make a square.
   (make square with other hand)

LINES

One straight finger makes a line.
   (hold up one index finger)
Two straight lines make one "t" sign.
   (cross index fingers)

Three lines made a triangle there
   (form triangle with index fingers touching
   and thumbs touching)
And one more line will make a square.
   (form square with hands)

DRAW A SQUARE

Draw a square, draw a square
Shaped like a tile floor.
Draw a square, draw a square
All with corners four.

DRAW A TRIANGLE

Draw a triangle, draw a triangle
With corners three.
Draw a triangle, draw a triangle
Draw it just for me.

DRAW A CIRCLE

Draw a circle, draw a circle
Made very round.
Draw a circle, draw a circle
No corners can be found.

WHAT AM I MAKING?

This is a circle.
   (draw circle in the air)
This is a square.
   (draw square in the air)

Who can tell me
What I'm making there?
    (draw another shape in the air)

Science:

1. **Feely Box**

    Cut many shapes out of different materials such as felt, cardboard, wallpaper, carpet, etc. Place the shapes into a feely box. The children can be encouraged to reach in and identify the shape by feeling it before removing it from the box.

2. **Evaporation**

    Pour equal amounts of water into a large round and a small square cake pan. Mark the water level with a grease pencil. Allow the water to stand for a week. Observe the amount of evaporation.

3. **Classifying Objects**

    Collect four small boxes. Mark a different shape on each box. Include a circle, triangle, square, and rectangle. Then cut shapes out of magazines. The children can sort the objects by placing them in the corresponding boxes.

4. **What Shape Is It?**

    Place objects with distinct shapes in the feely box such as marbles, dice, pyramid, deck of cards, book, ball, button, etc. Encourage the children to reach in and identify the shape of the object they are feeling before they pull it out.

Dramatic Play:

1. **Baker**

    Provide playdough, cake pans, and cookie cutters.

2. **Puppets**

    A puppet prop box should be placed in the dramatic play area. If available a puppet stage should be added. Otherwise a puppet stage can be made from cardboard.

Arts and Crafts:

1. **Sponge Painting**

    Cut sponges into the four basic shapes. The children can hold the sponges with a clothespin. The sponge can be dipped in paint and printed on the paper. Make several designs and shapes.

2. **Shape Mobiles**

    Trace shapes of various sizes on colored construction paper. If appropriate, encourage the children to cut the shapes from the paper and punch a hole at the top of each shape. Then, put a piece of string through the hole and tie onto a hanger. The mobiles can be hung in the classroom for decoration.

3. **Easel Ideas**

    Feature a different shape of easel paper each day at the easel.

4. **Shape Collage**

    Provide different-colored paper shapes and glue for the children to create collages from shapes.

5. **Stencils**

    Prepare individual stencils of the basic shapes. The children can use the stencils for tracing.

6. **My Shape Book**

    Stickers, catalogs, and magazines should be placed on the art table. Also, prepare booklets cut into the basic shapes. Encourage the children to find, cut, and glue the objects in each shape book.

Sensory:

Add the following items to the sensory table:

1. marbles and water
2. different-shaped sponges and water
3. colored water
4. scented water
5. soapy water

Large Muscle:

1. Walk and Balance

Using masking tape, outline the four basic shapes on the floor. The children can walk and balance on the shapes. Older children may walk forwards, backwards, and sideways.

2. Hopscotch

Draw a hopscotch with chalk on the sidewalk outdoors. Masking tape can be used to form the grid on the floor indoors.

Field Trip:

Shape Walk

Walk around the school neighborhood. During the walk, observe the shapes of the traffic signs and houses. After returning to the school, record the shapes observed on a chart.

Math:

1. Wallpaper Shape Match

From scraps of old wallpaper, cut out two sets of basic shapes. Then mix all of the pieces. The children can match the sets by pattern and shape.

2. Shape Completion

On several pieces of white tagboad draw a shape, leaving one side, or part of a circle, unfinished or dotted. Laminate the tagboard. The children can complete the shape by drawing with watercolor markers or grease pencils. Erase with a damp cloth.

Group Time (games, language):

1. Shape Hunt

Throughout the classroom hide colorful shapes. Each of the children can find a shape.

2. Twister

On a large old bed sheet, secure many shapes of different colors, or draw the shapes on with magic markers. Make a spinner. Have children place parts of their bodies on the different shapes.

3. Shape Day

Each day highlight a different shape. Collect related items that resemble the shape of the day and display throughout the classroom. During group time, have each child find an object in the classroom that is the same shape as the shape of the day.

Cooking:

1. Shaped Bread and Peanut Butter

The children can cut bread with different-shaped cookie cutters. Spread peanut butter or other toppings on the bread.

2. Fruit Cut-outs

1/2 cup sugar
4 envelopes unflavored gelatin
2 1/2 cups pineapple juice, apple juice, orange juice, grape juice, or fruit drink

In a mixing bowl, stir the sugar and gelatin with rubber scraper until well mixed. Pour fruit juice into a 1-quart saucepan. Put the pan on the burner. Turn the burner to high heat. Cook until the juice boils. Turn burner off. Pour boiling fruit juice over sugar mixture. Stir with a rubber scraper until all the gelatin is dissolved. Pour into a 13-inch x 9-inch x 2-inch pan. Place in the refrigerator and chill until firm. Cookie cutters can be used to make shapes. Enjoy! This activity requires close supervision.

3. Shape Snacks

Spread cheese or peanut butter onto various-shaped crackers and serve.
Serve cheese cut into circles, triangles, squares, and rectangles.

Serve vegetable circles—cucumbers, carrots, zucchini.
Cut fruit snacks into circles—bananas, grapefruit wedges, apple slices, grapes—serve.

4. **Nachos**

   4 flour tortillas
   3/4 cup grated cheese
   1/3 cup chopped green pepper (optional)

   With clean kitchen scissors, cut each tortilla into 4 or 6 triangle wedges. Place on a cookie sheet and sprinkle the tortilla wedges with the cheese. Garnish with green pepper if desired. Bake in a 350-degree oven for 4 to 6 minutes or until the cheese melts. Makes 16 to 20 nachos.

5. **Swedish Pancakes**

   3 eggs
   1 cup milk
   1 1/2 cups flour
   1 tablespoon sugar
   1/2 teaspoon salt
   4 tablespoons butter
   1 cup heavy cream
   2 tablespoons confectioner's sugar or a 12-ounce jar of fruit jelly

   Using a fork or whisk, beat the eggs lightly in a large mixing bowl. Add half the milk. Fold in the flour, sugar, and salt. Melt the butter and add it, the cream, and the remaining milk to the mixture. Stir well. Lightly grease a frying pan or griddle, and place it over medium-high heat on a hot plate or stove. Carefully pour small amounts of the mixture onto the frying pan or griddle. Cook until the pancakes are golden around the edges and bubbly on top. Turn the pancakes over with a spatula and cook until the other sides are golden around the edges. Remove to a covered plate. Repeat until all the mixture is used. Sprinkle pancakes lightly with confectioner's sugar, or spread fruit jelly over them. Makes 3 dozen pancakes.

TO TEACH MATH CONCEPTS

Before a child can learn the more abstract concepts of arithmetic, he must be visually, physically, and kinesthetically aware of basic quantitative concepts. Included could be:

Form Discrimination	over	middle
	under	near
circle	top	far
square	bottom	above
triangle	long	below
rectangle	short	many
	tall	few
Vocabulary	high	more
	low	less
big	thick	through
little	thin	around
small	front	fast
smaller	back	slow
large	behind	up
larger	all	down
heavy	none	most
light	some	least
in	first	
out	last	

Multimedia:

The following resources can be found in educational catalogs:

1. "Round in a Circle," *We All Live Together Series, Vol. 1* [record]. Youngheart Records.

2. "Shapes," *We All Live Together Series—Vol. 3* [record]. Youngheart Records.

3. *My World Is Round* [record]. Melody House Records.

4. *Mr. Al Sings Colors and Shapes* [record]. Melody House Records.

5. *Shapes in Action* [record]. Kimbo Records.

6. *Shapes* [30-minute video]. Edu-vid.

7. *Talking Stickybear Shapes* [Apple/IBM/IIGS software, PK–1]. Optimum Resources.

8. *Talking Stickbear Opposites* [Apple/IBM/IIGS software, PK–1]. Optimum Resources.

9. *Play & Learn Shapes* [IBM software, PK–1]. Remarkable.

10. *Learning My ABC's/Shapes* [video]. Tele-Story.

Books:

The following books can be used to complement the theme:

1. Hoban, Tana. (1986). *Shapes, Shapes, Shapes*. New York: Greenwillow Books.

2. Hill, Eric. (1986). *Spot Looks at Shapes*. New York: Putnam.

3. Mahan, Ben. (1992). *See a Circle*. New York: McClanahan Books.

4. Mahan, Ben. (1992). *See a Square*. New York: McClanahan Books.

5. Mahan, Ben. (1992). *See a Star*. New York: McClanahan Books.

6. Mahan, Ben. (1992). *See a Triangle*. New York: McClanahan Books.

7. Falwell, Cathryn. (1992). *Shape Space*. Boston: Houghton Mifflin.

8. Bradbury, Lynee. (1992). *Shapes and Colors*. Auburn, ME: Ladybird Books, Inc.

9. Callinan, Karen. (1992). *Rectangles*. Mankato, MN: Capstone Press, Inc.

10. Rikys, Bodel. (1993). *Red Bear's Fun with Shapes*. New York: Dial Books for Young Readers.

11. Pienkowski, Jan. (1989). *Shapes*. New York: Simon and Schuster Trade.

12. Bryant-Mole, K. (1991). *Shapes*. Tulsa, OK: EDC Publishing.

13. Hoban, Tana. (1992). *Spirals, Curves, Fanshapes, and Lines*. New York: Greenwillow Books.

14. Karlan, Bernie. (1992). *Shapes: Circle*. New York: Simon and Schuster Trade.

15. Karlan, Bernie. (1992). *Shapes: Square*. New York: Simon and Schuster Trade.

16. Karlan, Bernie. (1992). *Shapes: Triangle*. New York: Simon and Schuster Trade.

17. MacKinnon, Debbie. (1992). *What Shape?* New York: Dial Books for Young Readers.

18. Oliver, Stephen (Photog.). (1990). *My First Look at Shapes*. New York: David McKay Co.

19. Parramon, J. M. (1991). *My First Shapes*. Hauppauge, NY: Barron's Educational Series, Inc.

20. Weissman, Bari. (1992). *Dial Playshapes: Circles*. New York: Dial Books for Young Readers.

21. Weissman, Bari. (1992). *Dial Playshapes: Square*. New York: Dial Books for Young Readers.

22. Weissman, Bari. (1992). *Dial Playshapes: Triangle*. New York: Dial Books for Young Readers.

THEME 20

Equipment

balls
bats
shoulder pads
rackets
bikes
skis
boots
poles
gloves
helmets
golf clubs
skates

Places

yards
swimming pools
fields
tennis courts
roads
gyms
golf courses
bowling alleys
ski slopes
lakes

SPORTS

Types

baseball
basketball
football
soccer
rugby
swimming
tennis
volleyball
skiing
biking
bowling
skating
track/running
fishing
golf
hockey

Participants

spectators
players
coaches
umpires
scorekeepers
announcers

Clothing

uniforms
swimsuits
shorts
jerseys
sweatshirts
sweatpants
hats
ski clothing
jacket, gloves
pants, goggles

Theme Goals:

Through participating in the experiences provided by this theme, the children may learn:

1. Places used for sports participation.

2. Types of sports people play.

3. Types of equipment used for sports.

4. Kinds of clothing worn for sports participation.

5. There are many people who participate in sports.

Concepts for the Children to Learn:

1. Swimming pools, playing fields, tennis courts, roads, gyms, golf courses, backyards, bowling lanes, lakes, and ski slopes are all places that are used for sports.

2. Spectators, players, and coaches are all sports participants.

3. Baseball, biking, hockey, football, and golf are all types of sports.

4. Balls, bikes, and golf clubs are sports equipment.

5. Uniforms are worn when playing some sports.

6. Some sports are played indoors; others outdoors.

7. There are individual and team sports.

Vocabulary:

1. **team**—a group of people who play together.

2. **uniform**—clothing worn for some sports.

3. **ball**—equipment used for sports.

4. **sport**—an activity played for fun.

Bulletin Board

The purpose of this bulletin board is to have the children hang the numeral ball on the glove that has the corresponding number of dots. To prepare the bulletin board, construct baseball mitts out of brown tagboard. Attach dots starting with one on each of the gloves. The number of gloves prepared and dots will depend upon the developmental maturity of the children. Hang the gloves on the bulletin board. Next construct white baseballs. Write a numeral, starting with one, on each of the balls.

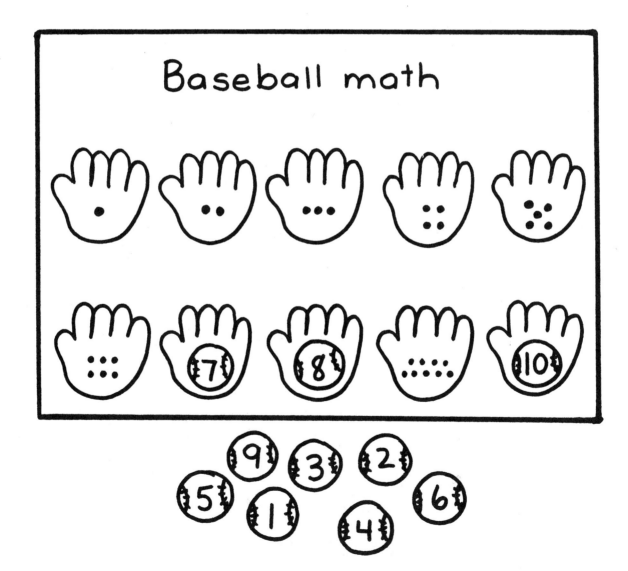

Parent Letter

Dear Parents,

Sports will be the focus of our next unit. Through the experiences provided, the children will become familiar with sports equipment and clothing. They will also recognize sports as a form of exercise.

At School

Activities planned to foster sports concepts include:

- exploring balls used in different sports and classifying them into groups by size, color, and ability to bounce and roll.
- trying on a variety of clothing used in different sports, including a swim cap, goggles, shoulder and leg/knee pads, helmets, gloves, and uniforms.
- skating in the room by wrapping squares of waxed paper around our feet and attaching them with rubber bands around our ankles. Our feet will then easily glide over the carpet!

At Home

You can incorporate sports concepts at home by:

- looking through sports magazines with your child and pointing out the equipment that is used or the clothing that is worn. This will develop your child's observation skills.
- observing a sporting event with your child, such as basketball, baseball, or football. Likewise, let your child watch you participate in a sport!
- participating in a sport together. Your child will enjoy spending special time with you!

Enjoy your child!

Soccer is a good physical activity.

Fingerplays:

HERE IS A BALL

Here's a ball
   (make a circle with your thumb and pointer
   finger)
And here's a ball
   (make a bigger circle with two thumbs and
   pointers)
And a great big ball I see.
   (make a large circle with arms)
Now let's count the balls we've made,
One, two, three.
   (repeat)

FOOTBALL PLAYERS

Five big football players standing in the locker
room door.
One had a sore knee
And then there were four.

Four big football players down on their knees.
One made a touchdown
And then there were three.

Three big football players looking up at you.
One made a tackle
And then there were two.

Two big football players running in the sun.
One was offsides
And then there was one.

One big football player standing all alone.
He decided to go home
And then there were none.

Science:

1. **Feely Box**

   Place a softball, hardball, golf ball, and tennis
   ball in a feely box. The children can reach into
   the box, feel, and try to guess the type of ball.

2. **Ball Bounces**

   Observe the way different balls move. Check
   to see if footballs, basketballs, and soccer balls
   can be bounced. Observe to see if some go
   higher than others. Also repeat using smaller
   balls such as tennis balls, baseballs, and golf
   balls.

3. **Wheels**

   Observe the wheels on a bicycle. If possible
   bring a bike to the classroom and demonstrate
   how peddling makes the wheels move.

4. **Examining Balls**

Observe the composition of different balls. Ask the children to identify each. Then place the balls in water. Observe to see which ones float and which ones sink.

5. **Types of Grass**

Place real grass and artificial turf on the science table. The children can feel both types of grass and describe differences in texture.

Dramatic Play:

1. **Baseball**

Baseball caps, plastic balls, uniforms, catcher's mask, and gloves can be placed in the dramatic play area.

2. **Football**

Balls, shoulder pads, uniforms, and helmets can be provided for the children to use outdoors.

3. **Tennis**

Tennis rackets, balls, visors, sunglasses, and shorts for the children can be placed outdoors. A variation would be to use balloons for balls and rackets made from hangers with a nylon pantyhose pulled around the hanger.

4. **Skiing**

Ski boots and skis can be provided for the children to try on.

5. **Skating**

Waxed paper squares for children to wrap around their feet and ankles can be provided. The children can attach the waxed paper with rubber bands around their ankles. Encourage the children to slide across the carpeting.

Arts and Crafts:

1. **Easel Ideas**

Cut easel paper in various sports shapes:

- baseball glove
- baseball diamond

- tennis racket
- bike
- tennis shoe
- football
- baseball cap
- football helmet
- all different sizes of balls

2. **Baseball Glove Lacing**

Prepare pre-cut baseball gloves out of brown construction paper. The older children might be able to cut them out themselves. Punch holes with a paper punch around the outer edge of the paper. Using yarn, let the children lace in and out of the holes of the gloves. Tie a knot at the end to secure the yarn.

3. **Collages**

Using sports-related magazines, encourage the children to cut out various pictures. These pictures can be pasted onto another piece of paper.

4. **Ball Collages**

Balls used in various sports come in all different sizes. Using construction paper or wallpaper, cut the paper in various round shapes, as well as football shapes. Encourage the children to paste them on a large piece of construction paper and decorate.

5. **Golf Ball Painting**

Place a piece of paper in a shallow tray or pie tin. Spoon two or three teaspoons of thin paint onto the paper. Then, put a golf ball or ping-pong ball in the tray and tilt the pan in a number of directions, allowing the ball to make designs in the paint.

Sensory:

1. **Swimming**

Add water to the sensory table with dolls or small people figures.

2. **Weighing Balls**

Fill the sensory table with small balls, such as golf balls, styrofoam balls, wiffle balls, or tennis balls. Add a balance scale so that the children can weigh the balls.

3. **Measuring Mud and Sand**

   Add a mud and sand mixture to the sensory table with scoops and spoons.

4. **Feeling Turf**

   Line the bottom of the sensory table with artificial turf.

Large Muscle:

1. **Going Fishing**

   Use a large wooden rocking boat or a large box that two to three children can sit in. Make fish out of construction paper or tagboard, and attach paper clips to the top. Tie a magnet to a string and pole. The magnet will attract the fish.

2. **Kickball**

   Many sports involve kicking a ball. Discuss these sports with the children. Then provide the children with a variety of balls to kick. Let the children discover which balls go the farthest and which are the easiest to kick.

3. **Sports Charades**

   Dramatize various sports including swimming, golfing, tennis, and bike riding.

4. **Golfing**

   Using a child-sized putter and regular golf balls, the children hit golf balls. This is an outdoor activity that requires a lot of teacher supervision.

5. **Beach Volleyball**

   Use a large beach ball and a rope or net in a central spot outdoors. Let the children volley the beach ball to one another.

Field Trips:

Suggested trips include:

1. a football field
2. a baseball field

3. tennis court
4. health (fitness) club
5. stadium
6. a swimming pool
7. the sports facilities of a local high school or college

Math:

1. **Ball Sort**

   Sort various balls by size, texture, and color.

2. **Hat Sorting**

   Sort hats such as baseball cap, football helmet, biking helmet, visor, etc., by color, size, texture, and shape.

Group Time (games, language):

"What's Missing?"

Provide the children in a large group with a tray of sports equipment such as a ball, baseball glove, golf ball, sunglasses, goggles, etc. Let the children examine the tray of items. Then have the children close their eyes and place their heads in their laps. Remove one item from the tray and see if the children can guess what is missing. This activity will be more successful if the numbers are related to the age of the child. For example, with two-year-old children, use only two items. Three-year-olds may be successful with an additional item. If not, remove one.

Cooking:

Cheese Balls

8 ounces cream cheese, softened
1 stick of butter, softened
2 cups grated cheddar cheese
1/2 package of onion soup mix

Blend all of the ingredients together. Shape the mixture into small balls. Roll the balls in chopped nuts if desired.

Multimedia:

The following resources can be found in educational catalogs:

1. *And the Beat Goes on for Physical Education* [record].

2. *Coordination Skills* [record].

3. *Exercise Is Kids' Stuff* [record].

4. *Fitness Fun for Everyone* [record].

5. *Have a Ball!* [record].

6. *Jumpnastics* [record].

Books:

The following books can be used to complement the theme:

1. Koda-Callan, Elizabeth. (1992). *Shiny Skates*. New York: Workman.

2. Kuklin, Susan. (1989). *Going to My Ballet Class*. New York: Macmillan.

3. Scioscia, Mary. (1993). *Bicycle Rider*. New York: Harper Collins.

4. Whitehead, Patricia. (1985). *Arnold Plays Baseball*. Mahwah, NJ: Troll.

5. Blackstone, Margaret. (1993). *This Is Baseball*. New York: Henry Holt.

6. Friend, David. (1992). *Baseball, Football, Daddy and Me*. New York: Puffin Books.

7. Riddle, Tohby. (1991). *Careful with That Ball, Eugene!* New York: Orchard Books.

8. Sanchez, Isidro, & Peris, Carme. (1992). *City Sports*. Hauppauge, NY: Barron's Educational Series, Inc.

9. Curtis, Gavin. (1990). *Grandma's Baseball*. New York: Crown Books for Young Readers.

10. Duffey, Betsy. (1992). *Lucky in Left Field*. New York: Simon and Schuster Trade.

11. McConnachie, Brian. (1992). *Elmer and the Chickens vs. the Big League*. New York: Crown Books for Young Readers.

12. Thayer, Ernest L. (1992). *Casey at the Bat*. New York: Putnam Publishing Group.

13. Real, Rory. (1990). *A Baseball Dream*. Hauppauge, NY: Barron's Educational Series, Inc.

14. Henderson, Kathy. (1991). *I Can Be a Basketball Player*. Chicago: Children's Press.

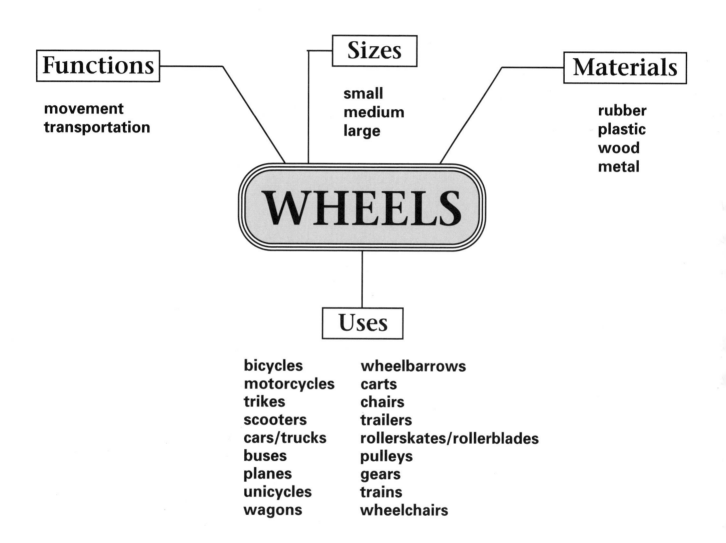

Functions

movement
transportation

Sizes

small
medium
large

Materials

rubber
plastic
wood
metal

WHEELS

Uses

bicycles
motorcycles
trikes
scooters
cars/trucks
buses
planes
unicycles
wagons

wheelbarrows
carts
chairs
trailers
rollerskates/rollerblades
pulleys
gears
trains
wheelchairs

Theme Goals:

Through participating in the experiences provided by this theme, the children may learn:

1. Sizes of wheels.

2. Purposes of wheels.

3. Materials used to make wheels.

4. Movement of wheels.

Concepts for the Children to Learn:

1. Wheels are round.

2. Wheels can help us to do our work.

3. Wheels help move people and things.

4. Cars, buses, motorcycles, and bicycles have wheels.

5. Wheels can be different sizes.

6. A unicycle is a one-wheeled cycle.

7. Wheels can be made of rubber, plastic, metal, or wood.

8. Wheels can be connected by an axle.

Vocabulary:

1. **wheel**—a form in the shape of a circle.

2. **unicycle**—a vehicle with one wheel.

3. **wheelbarrow**—a vehicle used for moving small loads.

4. **wheelchair**—a chair on wheels.

5. **bicycle**—a two-wheeled vehicle.

6. **pulley**—a wheel that can be connected to a rope to move things.

Bulletin Board

The purpose of this bulletin board is to encourage the development of mathematical concepts. To prepare the bulletin board, draw pictures of a unicycle, bicycle, and tricycle on tagboard. Color, cut out, and post on the bulletin board. Next, construct the numerals 1, 2, and 3 out of tagboard. Hang the numerals on the top of the bulletin board. A corresponding set of dots can be placed below the numeral to assist children in counting. A string can be attached to each numeral by using a stapler. Have the children wind the string around a push pin connected to the vehicle with the corresponding number of wheels.

Parent Letter

Dear Parents,

Wheels! Wheelchairs, wheelbarrows, tricycle wheels, bicycle wheels, and car wheels! Children see wheels almost every day of their lives. We will be studying wheels. Through participating in the activities planned for this unit, the children will discover that wheels can be made from many different materials and that there are many different uses and sizes of wheels.

At School

We have many learning experiences planned for this unit, which include:

- examining tire rubber at the science table.
- painting with toy cars at the art table.
- singing a song called, "The Wheels on the Bus."

At Home

There are many ways that you can incorporate this unit in your own home. Try any of these activities with your child.

- Walk around the neighborhood with your child. To develop observation skills look for different wheels.
- Count the wheels on the different types of transportation. Semi-trucks have several, while a unicycle has only one.
- Recite the following fingerplay with your child to foster language and memory skills. We will be learning it this week.

Wheels

Wheels big.
  (form big circles with fingers)
Wheels small.
  (form little circles with fingers)
Count them one by one.
Turning as they're pedaled
  (make pedaling motion with hands)
In the springtime sun!
1-2-3-4-5
  (count fingers)

Enjoy your child!

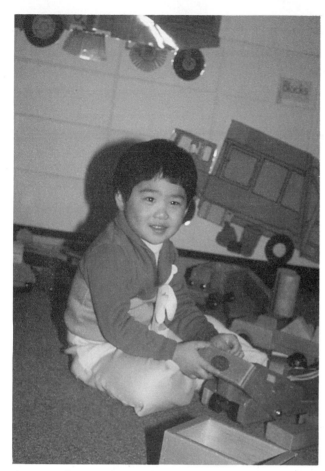

Cars and trucks need wheels to get around.

Music:

"The Wheels on the Bus"

The wheels on the bus go round and round,
Round and round, round and round.
The wheels on the bus go round and round
All through the town.

Other verses:
The wipers on the bus go swish, swish, swish.
The doors on the bus go open and shut.
The horn on the bus goes beep, beep, beep.
The driver on the bus says, "Move on back."
The people on the bus go up and down.

Fingerplays:

MY BICYCLE

One wheel, two wheels on the ground.
    (revolve hand in forward circle to form each
    wheel)

My feet make the pedals go round and round.
    (move feet in pedaling motion)
Handlebars help me steer so straight
    (pretend to steer bicycle)
Down the sidewalk, through the gate.

WHEELS

Wheels big.
    (form big circles with fingers)
Wheels small.
    (form little circles with fingers)
Count them one by one
Turning as they're pedaled
    (make pedaling motion with hands)
In the springtime sun.
1-2-3-4-5
    (count fingers)

Science:

1. **Tire Rubber**

    Cut off several pieces of rubber from old tires.
    Provide magnifying glasses. Encourage the
    children to observe similarities and differences.

2. **Pulley**

    Set up a pulley. Provide the children with
    blocks so they may lift a heavy load with the
    help of a wheel. Supervision may be necessary
    for this activity.

3. **Gears**

    Collect gears and place on the science table.
    The children can experiment, observing how
    the gears move. When appropriate, discuss
    their similar and different characteristics.

4. **Wheels and Axles**

    Set out a few wheels and axles. Discuss how
    they work as a lever to help lift heavy loads.
    Encourage the children to think about where
    they might find wheels and axles.

Dramatic Play:

1. **Car Mechanic**

    Outdoors, place various wheels, tires, tools,
    overalls, and broken trikes. The children can
    experiment using tools.

2. Floats

Paper, tape, crepe paper, and balloons can be provided to decorate the wheels on the tricycles, wagons, and scooters.

Arts and Crafts:

1. Circle Templates

Cut out various-sized circle templates from tagboard. Provide paper, pencils, and crayons for the children to trace the circles.

2. Car Painting

Provide small plastic cars, tempera paint, and paper. Place the tempera paint in a shallow pan. Car tracks can be created by dipping the car wheels in the tempera paint and rolling them across paper.

3. Wheel Collage

Provide magazines for the children to cut out pictures of wheels. The pictures can be pasted or glued onto sheets of paper.

4. Tracing Wheels

Provide sewing tracing wheels, pizza cutters, pastry wheels, carbon paper, and construction paper. The children can place the carbon paper on the construction paper and run one of the wheels over the carbon paper, making a design on the construction paper.

Sensory:

Sensory Table

Add the following items to the sensory table:

- sand with wheel molds
- rubber from tires
- gravel and small toy cars and trucks

Large Muscle:

1. Wheelbarrow

Place wheelbarrows in the play yard. Provide materials of varying weights for the children to move.

2. Wagons

Place wagons in the playground. Provide objects for the children to move.

Field Trips/Resource People:

1. Cycle Shop

Visit a cycle shop. Observe the different sizes of wheels that are in the shop. Talk about the different materials that wheels can be made of.

2. Machine Shop

Visit a machine parts shop. Look at the different gears, pulleys, and wheels. Discuss their sizes, shapes, and possible uses.

3. Resource People

- cycle specialist
- mechanic
- machinist
- person who uses a wheelchair

Math:

1. Wheel Sequence

Cut out various-sized circles from tagboard to represent wheels. The children can sequence the wheels from largest to smallest.

2. How Many Wheels?

Pictures of a unicycle, bicycle, tricycle, cars, scooters, and trucks of all sizes can be cut from magazines and catalogs. Mount the pictures on tagboard. Laminate. Sort the pictures according to the number of wheels.

Social Studies:

Wheelchair

Borrow wheelchair (child-sized if possible) from a local hospital or pharmacy. During group time discuss how wheelchairs help some people to move. Children can experience moving and pushing a wheelchair.

Group Time (games, language):

Who Took the Wheel?

(Variation of "Who Took the Cookie from the Cookie Jar")

Who took the wheel off the car today?
_____ took the wheel off the car today.
(fill _____ with a child's name)
Chosen child says, "Who me?"
Class responds, "Yes, you!"
Chosen child says, "Couldn't be!"
Class responds, "Well then, who?"

The chant continues as the chosen child picks another child. Continue repeating the chant using the children's names.

Cooking:

1. **Cheese Wheels**

   Cut cheese slices using a cookie cutter into circle shapes to represent wheels. Top the pieces with raisins or serve with crackers.

2. **Pizza Rounds**

   Provide each child with a half an English muffin. Demonstrate how to spread pizza sauce on a muffin. Then lay a few skinny strips of cheese across the top, making the cheese look like wheel spokes. Now let the children prepare their own. Bake in an oven at 350 degrees for 5 to 7 minutes or until the cheese melts. Cool slightly before serving.

Multimedia:

The following resources can be found in educational catalogs:

1. Raffi. "The Wheels on the Bus," *Rise and Shine* [record].

2. Penner, Fred. "Marvelous Toy," *Special Delivery* [record].

3. *The Bear's Bicycle* [video]. Live Oak Media.

Books:

The following books can be used to complement the theme:

1. Kovalski, Maryann. (1987). *The Wheels on the Bus: An Adaptation of the Traditional Song*. Boston: Little, Brown.

2. Crews, Donald. (1991). *Truck*. New York: Morrow.

3. Scioscia, Mary. (1993). *Bicycle Rider*. New York: Harper Collins.

4. Wolcott, Patty. (1991). *Double-Decker Double-Decker Double-Decker Bus*. New York: Random House.

5. Ziefert, Harriet. (1992). *Where's Daddy's Car?* New York: Harper Collins.

6. Ziefert, Harriet. (1992). *Where's Mommy's Truck?* New York: Harper Collins.

7. Pienkowski, Jan. (1992). *Wheels*. New York: Simon and Schuster Trade.

8. Stone, Venice. (1991). *Wheels*. New York: Scholastic Inc.

9. Strickland, Paul, & Flint, Russ. (1990). *Wheels at Work and Play* (6 vols). Milwaukee, WI: Gareth Stevens, Inc.

10. Dodds, Dayle A. (1989). *Wheel Away!* New York: Harper Collins Children's Books.

11. Hughes, Shirley. (1991). *Wheels*. New York: Lothrop, Lee, & Shepard Books.

12. Raffi. (1990). *Wheels on the Bus*. New York: David McKay Co.

13. Zelinsky, Paul O. (1990). *Wheels on the Bus: With Pictures That Move*. New York: Dutton Children's Books.

14. Rosen, Suri. (1992). *Wheels to Go: On the Go*. Los Angeles: Price Stern Sloan, Inc.

INTERNATIONAL HOLIDAYS

When planning the curriculum, it is important to note international holidays. The exact date of the holiday may vary from year to year; consequently, it is important to check with parents or a reference librarian at a local library. These international holidays for Christians, Buddhists, Eastern Orthodox, Hindus, Jews, and Muslims are as follows:

Christian

Ash Wednesday

Palm Sunday—the Sunday before Easter, which commemorates the triumphant entry of Jesus in Jerusalem.

Holy Thursday—also known as Maundy Thursday; it is the Thursday of Holy Week.

Good Friday—commemorates the crucifixion of Jesus.

Easter—celebrates the resurrection of Jesus.

Christmas Eve

Christmas Day—commemorates the birth of Jesus.

Buddhist

Nirvana Day (Mahayana Sect)—observes the passing of Sakyamuni into Nirvana. He obtained enlightenment and became a Buddha.

Magna Puja (Theravada Sect)—one of the holiest Buddhist holidays; it marks the occasion when 1,250 of Buddha's disciples gathered spontaneously to hear him speak.

Buddha Day (Mahayana Sect)—this service commemorates the birth of Gautama in Lumbini Garden. Amida, the Buddha of Infinite Wisdom and Compassion, manifested himself among men in the person Gautama.

Versakha Piya (Theravada Sect)—the most sacred of the Buddhist days. It celebrates the birth, death, and enlightenment of Buddha.

Maharram—marks the beginning of Buddhist Lent, it is the anniversary of Buddha's sermon to the first five disciples.

Vassana (Theravada Sect)—the beginning of the three-month period when monks stay in their temple to study and meditate.

Bon (Mahayana Sect)—an occasion for rejoicing in the enlightenment offered by the Buddha; often referred to as a "Gathering of Joy." Buddha had saved the life of the mother Moggallana. The day is in remembrance of all those who have passed away.

Pavarana (Theravada Sect)—celebrates Buddha's return to earth after spending one Lent season preaching in heaven.

Bodhi Day (Mahayana Sect)—celebrates the enlightenment of Buddha.

Eastern Orthodox

Christmas

First Day of Lent—begins a period of fasting and penitence in preparation for Easter.

Easter Sunday—celebrates the resurrection of Jesus.

Ascension Day—the 40th day after Easter, commemorates the ascension of Jesus to heaven.

Pentecost—commemorates the descent of the Holy Spirit upon the Apostles, 50 days after Easter Sunday. Marks the beginning of the Christian Church.

Hindu

Pongal Sankrandi—a three-day harvest festival.

Vasanta Pachami—celebrated in honor of Saraswati, the charming and sophisticated goddess of scholars.

Shivarari—a solemn festival devoted to the worship of Shiva, the most powerful of deities of the Hindu pantheon.

Holi—celebrates the advent of spring.

Ganguar—celebrated in honor of Parvari, the consort of Lord Shiva.

Ram Navami—birthday of the God Rama.

Hanuman Jayanti—birthday of Monkey God Humumanji.

Meenakshi Kalyanam—the annual commemoration of the marriage of Meenakshi to Lord Shiva.

Teej—celebrates the arrival of the monsoon; Parvari is the presiding deity.

Jewish

Yom Kippur—the most holy day of the Jewish year, it is marked by fasting and prayer as Jews seek forgiveness from God and man.

Sukkot—commemorates the 40-year wandering of Israelites in the desert on the way to the Promised Land; expresses thanksgiving for the fall harvest.

Simchat Torah—celebrates the conclusion of the public reading of the Pentateuch and its beginning anew, thus affirming that the study of God's word is an unending process. Concludes the Sukkot Festival.

Hanukkah—the eight-day festival that celebrates the rededication of the Temple to the service of God. Commemorates the Maccabean victory over Antiochus, who sought to suppress freedom of worship.

Purim—marks the salvation of the Jews of ancient Persia through the intervention of Queen Esther, from Haman's plot to exterminate them.

Passover—an eight-day festival marking ancient Israel's deliverance from Egyptian bondage.

Yom Hashoah—day of remembrance for victims of Nazi Holocaust.

Sahvout—celebrates the covenant established at Sinai between God and Israel and the revelation of the Ten Commandments.

Rosh Hashanah—the first of the High Holy Days marking the beginning of a ten-day period of penitence and spiritual renewal.

Muslim

Isra and Miraj—commemorates the anniversary of the night journey of the Prophet and his ascension to heaven.

Ramadan—the beginning of the month of fasting from sunrise to sunset.

Id al-Fitr—end of the month of fasting from sunrise to sunset; first day of pilgrimage to Mecca.

Hajj—the first day of pilgrimage to Mecca.

Day of Amfat—gathering of the pilgrims.

Id al-adha—commemorates the Feast of the Sacrifice.

Muharram—the Muslim New Year; marks the beginning of the Hedjra Year 1412.

Id al-Mawlid—commemorates the nativity and death of Prophet Muhammad and his flight from Mecca to Medina.

APPENDIX B

EARLY CHILDHOOD COMMERCIAL SUPPLIERS

ABC School Supply, Inc.
3312 N. Berkeley Lake Road
Delouth, Georgia 30136
(770) 497-0001

American Guidance Service
Publisher's Building
Circle Pines, Minnesota 55014
(612) 786-4343

Beckley Cardy
One East First Street
Duluth, Minnesota 55802
1-800-227-1178

Childcraft Educational Corporation
P.O. Box 3239
Lancaster, Pennsylvania 17604

Children's Press
5440 North Cumberland Avenue
Chicago, Illinois 60656
1-800-621-1115

Classic School Products
174 Semoran Commerce Place, Suite A106
Apopka, Florida 32703
1-800-394-9661

Community Playthings
Route 213
Rifton, New York 12471
(914) 658-8351

Constructive Playthings
1227 East 119th Street
Grandview, Missouri 64030-1117
1-800-832-0224

Cuisenaire Company of America, Inc.
12 Church Street, Box D
New Rochelle, New York 10802
1-800-237-3142

Delmar Publishers
3 Columbia Circle
Box 15-015
Albany, New York 12212-5015
1-800-998-7498

Didax Educational Resources
395 Main Street
Rowley, Massachusetts 01969
(508) 948-2340

Environments, Inc.
P.O. Box 1348
Beaufort, South Carolina 29901-1348
(803) 846-8155

Gryphon House, Inc.
3706 Otis Street
Mt. Rainier, Maryland 20712

The Highsmith Co., Inc.
W5527 Highway 106
P.O. Box 800
Fort Atkinson, Wisconsin 53538-0800
1-800-558-2110

J. L. Hammett
P.O. Box 9057
Braintree, Massachusetts 02184-9704
1-800-333-4600

Judy/Instructo
4325 Hiawatha Avenue
Minneapolis, Minnesota 55406

Kaplan School Supply Corporation
P.O. Box 609
Lewisville, North Carolina 27023-0609
1-800-334-2014

Kentucky School Supply
Dept. 21
P.O. Box 886
Elizabethtown, Kentucky 42702
1-800-626-4405

Kimbo Educational
10 North Third Avenue
Long Branch, New Jersey 07740
1-800-631-2187

Lakeshore Learning Materials
2695 E. Dominguez Street
Carson, California 90749
1-800-421-5354

Latta's School and Office Supplies
P.O. Box 128
2218 Main Street
Cedar Falls, Iowa 50613
(319) 266-3501

Nasco
901 Janesville Avenue
Fort Atkinson, Wisconsin 53538
1-800-558-9595

Primary Educator
1200 Keystone Avenue
P.O. Box 24155
Lansing, Michigan 48909-4155
1-800-444-1773

Redleaf Press
450 North Syndicate
Suite 5
St. Paul, Minnesota 55104-4125
(612) 641-6629

St. Paul Book and Stationery
1233 West County Road E
St. Paul, Minnesota 55112
1-800-338-SPBS (7727)

Valley School Supply
1000 North Bluemound Drive
P.O. Box 1579
Appleton, Wisconsin 54913
1-800-242-3433

Warren's Educational Supplies
980 West San Bernardino Road
Covina, California 91722-4196
(818) 966-1731

1. Get Acquainted Game

The children sit in a circle formation. The teacher begins the game by saying, "My name is ——— and I'm going to roll the ball to ———." Continue playing the game until every child has a turn. A variation of the game is have the children stand in a circle and bounce the ball to each other. This game is a fun way for the children to learn each other's names.

2. Hide the Ball

Choose several children and ask them to cover their eyes. Then hide a small ball, or other object, in an observable place. Ask the children to uncover their eyes and try to find the ball. The first child to find the ball hides it again.

3. "Which Ball is Gone?"

In the center of the circle, place six colored balls, cubes, beads, shapes, etc., in a row. Ask a child to close his eyes. Then ask another child to remove one of the objects and hide it behind him. The first child uncovers his eyes and tells which colored object is missing from the row. The game continues until all the selections have been made. When using with older children, two objects may be removed at a time to further challenge their abilities.

4. "What Sound is That?"

The purpose of this game is to promote the development of listening skills. Begin by asking the children to close their eyes. Make a familiar sound. Then ask a child to identify it. Sources of sound may include:

tearing paper	blowing a pitch pipe	raising or lowering
sharpening a pencil	dropping an object	window shades
walking, running,	moving a desk or	leafing through
shuffling feet	chair	book pages
clapping hands	snapping fingers	cutting with
sneezing, coughing	blowing nose	scissors
tapping on glass,	opening or closing	snapping rubber
wood, or metal	drawer	bands
jingling money	stirring paint in	ringing a bell
opening a window	a jar	clicking the tongue
pouring water	clearing the throat	crumpling paper
shuffling cards	splashing water	opening a box
blowing a whistle	rubbing sandpaper	sighing
banging blocks	together	stamping feet
bouncing ball	chattering teeth	rubbing palms
shaking a rattle	sweeping sound,	together
turning the lights on	such as a brush or	rattling keys
knocking on a door	broom	

A variation of this game could be played by having a child make a sound. Then the other children and the teacher close their eyes and attempt to identify the sound. For older children this game can be varied with the production of two sounds. Begin by asking the children if the sounds are the same or different. Then have them identify the sounds.

5. "Near or Far?"

The purpose of this game is to locate sound. First, tell the children to close their eyes. Then play a sound recorded on a cassette tape. Ask the children to identify the sound as being near or far away.

6. Descriptions

The purpose of this game is to encourage expressive language skills. Begin by asking each child to describe himself. Included with the description can be the color of his eyes, hair, and clothing. The teacher might prefer to use an imaginative introduction such as: "One by one, you may take turns sitting up here in Alfred's magic chair and describe yourself to Alfred." Another approach may be to say, "Pretend that you must meet somebody at a very crowded airport who has never seen you before. How would you describe yourself so that the person would be sure to know who you are?"

A variation for older children would be to have one of the children describe another child without revealing the name of the person he is describing. To illustrate, the teacher might say, "I'm thinking of someone with shiny red hair, blue eyes, many freckles, etc...." The child being described should stand up.

7. Mirrored Movements

The purpose of this game is to encourage awareness of body parts through mirrored movements. Begin the activity by making movements. Encourage the children to mirror your movements. After the children understand the game, they may individually take the leader role.

8. Little Red Wagon Painted Red

As a prop for the game, cut a red wagon with wheels out of construction paper. Then cut rectangles the same size as the box of the red wagon. Include purple, blue, yellow, green, orange, brown, black, and pink colors.

Sing the song to the tune of **"Skip to My Lou."**

*Little red wagon painted **red.***
*Little red wagon painted **red.***
*Little red wagon painted **red.***
What color would it be?

Give each child a turn to pick and name a color. As the song is sung, let the child change the wagon color.

9. Police Officer Game

Select one child to be the police officer. Ask him to find a lost child. Describe one of the children in the circle. The child who is the police officer will use the description as a clue to find the "missing child."

10. Mother Cat and Baby Kits

Choose one child to be the mother cat. Then ask the mother cat to go to sleep in the center of the circle, covering his eyes. Then choose several children to be kittens. The verse below is chanted as the baby kittens hide in different parts of the classroom. Following this, the mother cat hunts for them. When all of the kittens have been located, another mother cat may be selected. The number of times the game is repeated depends upon the children's interest and attention span.

Mother cat lies fast asleep.

To her side the kittens creep.

But the kittens like to play.

Softly now they creep away.

Mother cat wakes up to see.

No little kittens. Where can they be?

11. Memory Game

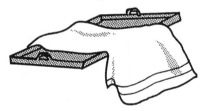

Collect common household items, a towel, and tray. Place the items on the tray. Show the tray containing the items. Cover with a towel. Then ask the children to recall the names of the items on the tray. To ensure success, begin the activity with only two or three objects for young children. Additional objects can be added depending upon the developmental maturity of the children.

12. Cobbler, Mend My Shoes

Sit the children in a circle formation. Then select one child to sit in the center. This child gives a shoe to a child in the circle, and then closes his eyes. The children in the circle pass the shoe around behind them while the rhyme is chanted. When the chant is finished, the shoe is no longer passed. The last child with the shoe in his hand holds the shoe behind his back. Then the child sitting in the center tries to guess who has the shoe.

Cobbler, cobbler, mend my shoe

Have it done by half past two

Stitch it up and stitch it down

Now see with whom the shoe is found.

13. Huckle Buckle Beanstalk

Ask the children to sit in a circle. Once seated, tell them to close their eyes. Then hide a small ball in an obvious place. Say, "Ready." Encourage all of the children to hunt for the object. Each child who spots it returns to a place in the circle and says, "Huckle buckle beanstalk." No one must tell where he has seen the ball until all the children have seen it.

14. What's Different?

Sit all of the children in a circle formation. Ask one child to sit in the center. The rest of the children are told to look closely at the child sitting in the center. Then the children are told to cover their eyes while you change some detail on the child in the center. For example, you may place a hat on the child, untie his shoe, remove a shoe, roll up one sleeve, etc. The children sitting in the circle act as detective to determine "what's different?"

15. Cookie Jar

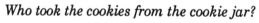

Sit the children in a circle formation on the floor with their legs crossed. Together they repeat a rhythmic chant while using alternating leg-hand clap to emphasize the rhythm. The chant is as follows.

Someone took the cookies from the cookie jar.

Who took the cookies from the cookie jar?

Mary took the cookies from the cookie jar.

Mary took the cookies from the cookie jar?

Who, me? (Mary)

Yes, you. (all children)

Couldn't be. (Mary)

Then who? (all children)

——————— *took the cookies from the cookie jar.* (Mary names another child.)

Use each child's name.

16. Hide and Seek Tonal Matching

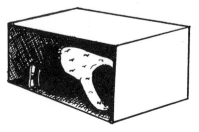

Sit the children in a circle formation. Ask one child to hide in the room while the other children cover their eyes. The children in the circle sing, "Where is ————— hiding?" The child who is hiding responds by singing back, "Here I am." With their eyes remaining closed, the children point in the direction of the hiding child. All open eyes and the child emerges from his hiding place.

17. Listening and Naming

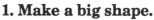

This game is most successful with a small group of children. The children should take turns shutting their eyes and identifying sounds as you tap with a wooden dowel on an object such as glass, triangle, drum, wooden block, cardboard box, rubber ball, etc.

18. Funny Shapes

Ask each child to choose a partner. One partner must make a large shape with his body. The other partner must follow the directions of movement. Roles reverse for the second set of directions. Provide directions such as:

1. Make a big shape.

go **over**
go **under**
go **through**
go **around**

2. Make a small shape.

go **over**
go **under**
go **through**
go **around**

19. Drop the Handkerchief

Direct the children to stand in a circle formation. Ask one child to run around the outside of the circle, dropping a handkerchief behind another child. The child who has the handkerchief dropped behind him must pick it up and chase the child who dropped it. The first child tries to return to the vacated space by running before he is tagged.

20. "If You Please"

This game is a simple variation of "Simon Says." Ask the children to form a circle around a leader who gives directions, some of which are prefaced with "if you please." The children are to follow only the "if you please" directions, ignoring any that do not begin with "if you please." Directions to be used may include walking forward, hopping on one foot, bending forward, standing tall, etc. This game can be varied by having the children follow the directions when the leader says, "do this," and not when he says, "do that." Play only one version of this game on a single day. Too much variety will confuse the children.

21. Duck Duck Goose	Ask the children to squat in a circle formation. Then ask one child to walk around the outside of circle, lightly touching each child's head and saying "Duck, Duck." When he touches another child and says "Goose," that child chases him around the circle. If the child who was "it" returns to the "goose's" place without being tagged, he remains. When this happens, the tapped child is "it." This game is appropriate for older four-, five-, six-, and seven-year-old children.
22. Fruit Basket Upset 	Ask the children to sit in a circle formation on chairs or on carpet squares. Then ask one child to sit in the middle of the circle as the chef. Hand pictures of various fruits to the rest of the children. Then to continue the game, ask the chef to call out the name of a fruit. The children holding that particular fruit exchange places. If the chef calls out, "fruit basket upset," all of the children must exchange places, including the chef. The child who doesn't find a place is the new chef. A variation of this game would be bread basket upset. For this game use pictures of breads, rolls, bagels, muffins, breadsticks, etc. This game is appropriate for older children.
23. Bear Hunt 	This is a rhythmic chant which may easily be varied. Start by chanting each line, encouraging the children to repeat the line. **Teacher:** *Let's go on a bear hunt.* **Children:** *(Repeat. Imitate walk by slapping knees alternately.)* **Teacher:** *I see a wheat field.* *Can't go over it;* *Can't go under it.* *Let's go through it.* (arms straight ahead like you're parting wheat) *I see a bridge.* *Can't go over it;* *Can't go under it.* *Let's swim.* (arms in swimming motion) *I see a tree.* *Can't go over it;* *Can't go under it.* *Let's go up it.* (climb and look) *I see a swamp.* *Can't go over it;* *Can't go under it.* *Let's go through it.* (pull hands up and down slowly) *I see a cave.* *Can't go over it;* *Can't go under it.* *Let's go in.* (walking motion) *I see two eyes. I see two ears.* *I see a nose. I see a mouth.* *It's a BEAR!!!* (Do all in reverse very fast)

200

24. "Guess Who?"

Individually tape the children's voices. Play the tape during group time, and let the children identify their classmates' voices.

25. Shadow Fun

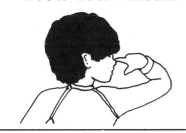

Hang a bed sheet up in the classroom for use as a projection screen. Then place a light source such as a slide, filmstrip, or overhead projector a few feet behind the screen. Ask two of the children to stand behind the sheet. Then encourage one of the two children to walk in front of the projector light. When this happens, the children are to give the name of the person who is moving.

26. If This Is Red— Nod Your Head

Point to an object in the room and say, "If this is green, shake your hand. If this is yellow, touch your nose." If the object is not the color stated, children should not imitate the requested action.

27. Freeze

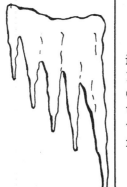

Encourage the children to imitate activities such as washing dishes, cleaning house, dancing, etc. Approximately every 10 to 20 seconds, call out "Freeze!" When this occurs, the children are to stop whatever they are doing and remain frozen until you say, "Thaw" or "Move." A variation of this activity would be to use music. When the music stops, the children freeze their movements.

28. Spy the Object

Designate a large area on the floor as home base. Then select an object and show it to the children. Ask the children to cover their eyes while you place the object in an observable place in the room. Then encourage the children to open their eyes and search for the object. As each child spies the object he quietly returns to the home base area without telling. The other children continue searching until all have found the object. After all the children are seated, they may share where the object is placed.

29. Who Is Gone?

This game is played in a circle format. Begin by asking a child to close his eyes. Then point to a child to leave the circle and go to a spot where he can't be seen. The child with his eyes closed opens them at your word, then looks around the circle and identifies the friend who is missing.

30. It's Me

Seat the children in a circle formation, and place a chair in the center. Choose one child to sit on a chair in the circle, closing his eyes. After this, ask another child to walk up softly behind the chair and tap the child on the shoulder. The seated child asks, "Who is tapping?" The other child replies, "It's me." By listening to the response, the seated child identifies the other child.

31. Feeling and Naming

Ask a child to stand with his back to you, placing his hands behind him. Then place an object in the child's hands for identification by feeling it. Nature materials can be used such as leaves, shells, fruit, etc. A ball, doll, block, Lego piece, puzzle piece, crayon, etc., may also be used.

32. Doggy, Doggy, Where's Your Bone?

Sit the children in a circle formation. Then place a chair in the center of the circle. Place a block under the chair. Select one child, the dog, to sit on the chair and close his eyes. Then point to another child. This child must try to get the dog's bone from under the chair without making a noise. After the child returns to his place in the circle, all the children place their hands behind them. Then in unison the children say, "Doggy, Doggy, where's your bone?" During the game, each dog has three guesses as to who has the bone.

202

Index by Subject